The Dead Are Talking

By Ross Hemsworth

The Dead Are Talking by Ross Hemsworth
Copyright © 2007 by Reality Press
All rights reserved.

No part of this book may be reproduced or transmitted in any form or by any means, graphic, electronic, or mechanical, including photocopying, recording, taping or by any information storage or retrieval system, without permission in writing from the publisher at: info@reality-entertainment.com.

Reality Press
An imprint of Reality Entertainment, Inc.

For information contact:

REALITY ENTERTAINMENT
P.O. Box 91
Foresthill, CA 95631

ph: 530-367-5389, fx: 530-367-3024

www.reality-entertainment.com

ISBN: 0-9791750-2-X

Foreword

Dedicated to the woman who turned my life around
"Penny Dando" with all my love.

For centuries the words "paranormal" or "occult" have been associated with words such as insanity, mental illness and even "evil". But now, evidence is beginning to emerge that could show paranormal researchers as nearer reality than the skeptical community!

Let's not forget that the word "paranormal" is merely that which cannot currently be scientifically explained as "normal". It does not necessarily mean that someone that researches it believes in ghosts! Electricity may have been deemed paranormal before it was fully explained by science.

There are many things we do not understand in our world and in the universe around us. How many times has the question arisen "what came first, the chicken or the egg?" yet so far, no-one has been able to answer that particular conundrum.

What is at the end of space? As humans we have a real problem with infinity, it just doesn't make sense to our somewhat limited brain capability. We imagine the end of space as something like a brick wall, but as that only has limited thickness, what is behind that brick wall? It's enough to blow a complete set of brain fuses! But could it be that the brain was designed only for our relatively short time on Earth in our physical body? Maybe it just wasn't designed to understand the many mysteries of the universe. Imagine the brain purely as the RAM of your bodily computer or the virtual memory.

Perhaps our "mind" is completely separate from the brain, and like your computer's hard drive, has a much larger storage capacity, and maybe we can "tap into the server network" or a universal consciousness which allows us to explore much further.

In this book, I will put forward my own views, ideas and evidence from my research which just may make you think again about what and HOW your belief system works.

I was not convinced of the existence of the paranormal by one singular event, but by many events over several years – yet skeptics expect us to convince them with one solid piece of evidence on a single investigation – it just doesn't work like that! So my job is not to convince the skeptics, it is purely to ask you to open your mind to possibilities that you may not have thought about before. I want you to think without boundaries, and dismiss nothing until you have witnessed it for yourself.

I estimate that 90% of alleged paranormal occurrences, have logical and rational explanations, but the 10% that will not fit into that particular box, is what began my quest for answers. Although I must add, that for every answer one gets in paranormal research, it tends to produce a further ten questions.

This book is not however, just about GHOSTS! In the following chapters I deal with many subjects including UFO's, parallel dimensions, dowsing, ley lines, Earth energies, The Knights Templars and even my own thoughts of suicide after my divorce! My journey and quest for the truth has not been an easy one. Be warned – enter the world of paranormal research at your own risk – it can be fraught with danger, anguish, verbal and physical attacks from others and even an ear-battering from religious groups.

Please remember as you read through the following pages, that I started my quest as a skeptic and was not easily convinced of the existence of the paranormal realm.

I also talk about some of the guests on my radio show "Now THAT'S Weird" as many have made ME think again about what I actually believe. If you are a listener to the programme which airs on Friday nights on Net Talk Radio (www.nettalkradio.co.uk), you will know how addictive the programme is, and how the different guests each week present new evidence and facts that many of us find intriguing.

I also take aim at the Church and various religions in the book, although I myself do believe in God, but I believe the worst thing that ever happened to Christianity was Christians themselves who have chosen what gospels we should and shouldn't see, and have changed the wording of original texts to "police the masses". Yes, its controversial – but I believe it's time we stood up and said what we really think. If you want to talk to God – do you really need to go to a special building to do it, a building often full of many hypocrites?

But it's not only the Christians that come in for attack – what about religious groups that believe in killing, murder and wars in the name of God or Allah?

My journey has taken me around the world, and I have met some amazing people including Doctors J.J. and Desiree Hurtak (The Keys of Enoch) – people who have shown me that there is so much more than the physical world around us.

I was once someone who wore only top name designer clothes such as Armani and Versace, I owned a Mercedes Benz with my initials on the number plate and I wanted the best things in life – but these were all physical things of little worth beyond our 70 or so years in human form! Now, I have distanced myself from materialism and look towards a spiritual path that may give me far greater worth in the existence yet to come. Don't get me wrong, we all need to make a living to pay the bills, but physical wealth brings only heartache, whereas spiritual wealth offers so much more.

So all I ask is that you read my research, study my journey through some incredibly good and bad times, with an open mind and allow yourself to be open to some new thinking, new ideas and explanations for things that you may have previously taken for granted.

Chapters

Introduction	*1 - 2*
Chapter 1 - Humble Beginnings	*3 - 8*
Chapter 2 - Ghost Detectives	*9 - 18*
Chapter 3 – Affairs, Separations, Divorce and Ghosts!	*19 - 23*
Chapter 4 – Other Reasons for Paranormal Activity?	*25 - 27*
Chapter 5 – My First Meeting with Dr. Sam Parnia	*29 - 32*
Chapter 6 - The Colchester Incident	*33 - 35*
Chapter 7 – The Tower of London Live!	*37 - 39*
Chapter 8 - The New Jersey Vortex	*41 - 43*
Chapter 9 – Working with Other Organizations	*45 - 47*
Chapter 10 – Light & Sound Frequency Phenomena	*49 - 51*
Chapter 11 – Telepathy & ESP	*53 - 56*
Chapter 12 – Orbs - The Greatest Debate in Years	*57 - 60*
Chapter 13 – EVP – Voices of the Dead?	*61 - 63*
Chapter 14 – TV's Love of the Sceptics	*65 - 67*
Chapter 15 - My Clash with James Randi & His Followers	*69 - 71*
Chapter 16 – Re-incarnation – Surely Not Another 70 Years?	*73 - 75*
Chapter 17 – So You're Dead, Why Come Back Here?	*77 - 80*
Chapter 18 – Parallel Dimensions – An Answer or a Confusion?	*81 - 84*
Chapter 19 – Dowsing When is a Ley Line NOT a Ley Line?	*85 - 88*

Chapter 20 – Investigations - Moments that Changed My Thinking   89 - 100

Chapter 21 – UFO's, Aliens & Abductions   101 - 102

Chapter 22 – The Knights Templars – Another Quest?   103 - 107

Chapter 23 – Children & Sensitivity   109 - 110

Chapter 24 - A United Paranormal Research World? Unlikely   111 - 112

Chapter 25 - The Hitchhikers Guide to Haunting!   113 - 120

Chapter 26 – Physical Mediumship   121 - 124

Chapter 27 - The Church & Its Effect on Us   125 - 127

Chapter 28 – The End of the World is Nigh! Not Bloody Likely!   129 - 131

Chapter 29 - Working Towards a New Future for Paranormal Research   133 - 136

Chapter 30 – The Guests on My Radio Show Who Have Opened My Mind   137 - 145

Chapter 31 - Conclusions   147 - 150

Introduction

My story begins in 1998. I was running a small struggling TV production company in Dunstable in Bedfordshire. Another day had begun, much like the rest, with a series of programme proposal rejections from the likes of ITV, BBC and Channel 4 and the usual pile of overdue payment reminders.

Suddenly the office door opened and in walked a fully uniformed Police Officer! My first thought was "oops, must have forgot about the parking restrictions outside again". Hi, he said, my name is Graham Matthews and I wondered if I could talk to you about ghosts. As an ardent sceptic at the time I replied, you can talk about whatever you like if it stops you from being outside ticketing my car.

It turned out that Graham was also a sceptic, who had been invited to attend a number of paranormal investigations as a photographer (his hobby) with a local group of ghost-hunters and had devised what he thought would make a good TV series about the subject. He was totally deflated when I said that it had all been done before, and there was no requirement for such programmes on TV.

He went on to persuade me however, that I should attend a couple of these overnight investigations before closing the door completely, and after several cups of tea and much persuasion, I grudgingly agreed.

Over the next few months, Graham and I attended a number of local paranormal investigations, and I was astonished at just how prehistoric their research methods were! In short, a group of people huddled up on the floor of a cold, damp, dark building throughout the night, awaiting the appearance of an ectoplasmic entity, who would shake their hand and say "Hi, I'm Fred and I'm dead". They wanted what all ghost-hunters seem to seek, solid proof of what I have come to call the "Hollywood Ghost" – a full body, solid walking and talking apparition. If only it were that easy.

I decided that there must be a better way to attempt to prove or disprove the existence of any form of "paranormal activity", and invested heavily in a range of new hi-tech monitoring equipment, and arranged a series of scientific experiments, and together with Graham, formed The Phantom or Fraud Project. The paranormal quest had begun, little did I know at that point in time, how it was to change my entire life, help to break up my marriage and lead me on a journey to try to prove soul survival beyond human physical death.

www.phantomorfraud.org

One
Humble Beginnings

The first investigations we carried out, were admittedly, quite disorganised and failed to provide us with any real evidence of paranormal activity, although Graham did get momentarily excited by a "floating ball of light" he monitored moving around a bar of a public house we were investigating in the early hours of a Sunday morning, only to find he was monitoring a reflection of the headlight of a maneuvering car in the car park outside!

Much of what is found on a normal paranormal investigation, can be easily explained rationally and logically, and we therefore decided that elimination of the "obvious" and "seemingly obvious" would be a good starting point for any alleged activity. For example if a door suddenly bangs shut, could it have been caused by a draught? If a voice is recorded on tape that is not one of the team, could it be people walking past outside, or a chance recording of a freak radio wave from a local taxi rank.

Neither Graham nor I were wealthy people, and within our first few weeks, we were already starting to wonder how we could continue to finance these investigations.

It was at this point that I said to Graham, perhaps if we COULD get the broadcasters interested in what we were doing, the money from the programmes could fund the actual research of the Project.

For several months, we ploughed idea after idea into the TV commissioner's offices only to receive rejection after rejection of the varying ideas we had put forward. We were both beginning to feel that this was just never going to work. One snooty former terrestrial commissioner even said "darling, this is SO not me, ghosts do not exist everyone knows that and I will not subject our viewers to such rubbish"! She left the channel a short while after.

Our early investigations however, were showing that whilst 95% of alleged "activity" WAS easily explainable, there was a nagging 5% which defied explanation, and I found this intriguing and extremely addictive.

We then hit on the idea of "membership", recruiting other people to join us on investigations, paying an annual fee to be part of the organization. We designed and launched a web site and offered others the chance to come and work with us, and to our surprise the money started to trickle in.

With the money, came new minds, new ideas, and people with their own ghost-hunting equipment, all of which helped us to grow quickly and become established as a major force in scientific paranormal research in the UK. We created a non-for-profit organization and all the income was ploughed back into the research

Over the coming months, it became obvious to us, that a single night at an alleged haunted location, was not enough. Many of our original investigations were at haunted pubs which were never empty and ready for our work until well after midnight, then, having spent two to three hours setting up equipment, there wasn't much of the night left to actually carry out a paranormal investigation. We made a decision at that time, that we needed to carry out longer monitored investigations.

Also, by this time, the pressure was starting to show in my home life. My wife at the time Irene (known as Kathy because of an attempted singing career earlier in her life) was complaining about me spending a lot of my spare time in building Phantom or Fraud and began warning me that if I was spending weekends away, she would too. She would ring me at investigations and tell me that one of the kids was ill just to get me to come home only to find that it was no more than a common cold. One of my colleagues had even commented "when she says jump Ross – you say how high". She was telling everyone I was into the "occult". Now whilst in dictionary terms it is a correct description, the term itself conjures up pictures of dark practices and devil-worship to friends and neighbors and I certainly had no interest in that.

In 2000, Graham and I launched our largest investigation to date at the allegedly haunted Dalston Hall Hotel on the edge of the Lake District. With the kind cooperation of the owners, we took a team of around a dozen people, including clairvoyants and dowsers and set-up a week-long investigation of the building. The results were to change the very way investigations were carried out by the Project.

My first direct encounter with something that may be called "paranormal" was two weeks before the investigation, when I went up on my own to do a "recce". A recce is a TV term for a pre-visit where you see what equipment and lighting may be needed, measure cable and camera requirements and check for possible problems that may be encountered, to save time at the actual investigation.

I booked myself into Room 4 – allegedly the most haunted room at the hotel, or so I was told by the management, who seemed somewhat surprised that I actually WANTED to spend a night in there on my own!

I set up a camera and infrared light in the room at the far end by the window, monitoring the whole area, and facing the door – the only entrance in and out of the accommodation. This was connected to a small VHS recorder and put on slow speed, thus allowing a four hour VHS tape to run for around 8 hours. It was 2200 hours, and the video was now filming. I decided to leave the room at this point and head for the bar for some "Dutch courage" before the long night ahead, alone in the room. Yes, I WAS a sceptic, but it's funny just how the slightest draught, noise or other sound, cause the hairs to stand up on one's neck!

I returned about an hour and a half later, checked that the video was still recording, and then went to the bathroom to do the usual pre-bed routine. I then put myself to bed and slept until around 2 a.m. when I was abruptly awoken by what I can only describe as a "hand" touching my inner thigh. Now if this was some gorgeous female I had met in the bar, I may have not been quite so alarmed, but whilst feeling the hand, I could see NO-ONE THERE!

The hand then seemed to move up my thigh and touch my genitals at which point I leaped from the bed to switch on a light. I have to say at this point, I was shaking like a leaf. Could I have dreamt such an occurrence, well the video would certainly prove that in the morning. (Or so I thought.)

With the light on, the atmosphere in the room changed, and after making myself a coffee, I decided that it MUST have been my imagination, and returned to sleep eventually (with the lamp left ON.).

Nothing else occurred that night to my knowledge, yet I was awoken at 0730 hours by the sound of the VHS recorder switching itself off. Now to my estimation, a tape capable of capturing only 8 hours of filming, and switched-on at 2200 hours the night before, SHOULD have gone off automatically at 0600 hours, so I was a little intrigued, and decided to have a quick look back at what was on the tape.

To my utter amazement, I saw myself leave the room to go to the bar, shortly after setting the camera up, yet my next appearance was coming OUT of the bathroom! There was no jump in the film as if the equipment had gone off and switched back on, and even then if there was a power-cut, it would not come back on automatically, it would have gone into standby mode. So why did it not show me re-entering the room?

I forwarded through the tape and again to my amazement, there was NO POINT where I had got out of bed and made a coffee, yet the bedroom light did come on at what would have been around 0300 hours! (This would have been the approximate time I retuned to bed after the "incident"). I thought about it and convinced myself that it must have been a dream, and whilst the light coming on by itself was strange, maybe it was some kind of power surge. I decided therefore, to study the tape in far more depth when I retuned back to the office.

I made my way downstairs for breakfast before checking out, and asked the young lady at reception, what kind of "paranormal things" had been reported previously in Room 4. You could have knocked me down with a feather when she replied "well men sleeping alone in there, have often reported that they have been touched intimately by a hand in the night". Luckily, she added that the alleged ghost WAS a female.

Upon arrival back in Dunstable, I called Graham and the two of us watched through the tape, and to our astonishment, it appears to go off at around 0145 hours and back on again at around 0315 hours, but with no usual signs of "noise" the "snow effect" associated with the switching on and off of a VHS recorder during filming. This was the documented time of the alleged paranormal activity.

We discussed at length, things like power-cuts and power-surges, but NONE would allow the video to come back on in record mode. This would however, explain the recording length of the tape finishing at 0730 hours instead of 0600 hours.

We decided we would tell no-one on the team about this event, or about which rooms at the Dalston were supposedly haunted so that we could monitor other possible occurrences during the main investigation, so imagine our surprise when another team member experienced virtually the same thing in Room 4 during the stake-out! The same investigator also had a laptop computer go off whilst using it, which he decided must have been a power cut or fuse gone. After returning from the toilet, the computer was back on with the programme displayed that he had been previously working on. No-one in the room had rebooted it!

Our first real encounter with the phenomena known as "orbs", also happened during this investigation. Orbs are small balls of light that seem to appear in mainly digital photographs and on night-vision cameras under infrared conditions.

There are many theories about what orbs may be, which include out-of-focus points of light such as dust, pollen or moisture in the air, caught by the flash of the camera or an infrared light source, but our experiments seem to discount these theories for reasons I will go into later in this book.

The thing that has always fascinated me about orbs is that they usually appear in the exact spot where clairvoyants are telling you they see a "spirit", and clairvoyants and sensitives seem to have far more success in photographing or filming these anomalies, than the sceptics! Surely if it were dust, pollen or moisture, we would ALL photograph them, and they would even be in our holiday pictures, so WHY just in haunted houses?

Marion Goodfellow was our lead clairvoyant in the early days of Phantom, and was probably the ONLY clairvoyant who ever really convinced me that clairvoyance wasn't just a trick or scam. Over and over again Marion came up with information that she could not have known before an investigation, as she had not even been told where she was being taken. I believed this woman had a real gift.

At Dalston, Marion successfully predicted the appearance of a "spirit" time and time again in our photographs, and often, these orbs would appear in the exact spot where she would tell us a "spirit" was standing. The best evidence came when she and other sensitives, were "moving a spirit into the light" outside in the grounds of the Dalston Hotel, late one night towards the end of the investigation. Graham took a picture on his Nikon Coolpix Digital Camera and the flash failed to go off. Yet in the pitch darkness, there was an orb appearing to leave the medium's circle.

At the end of the Dalston Hall investigation, we held a debrief in the presence of the owners, who only then told us of some of the strange occurrences experienced before. To their amazement, Marion and her clairvoyant team had picked up on ALL of these alleged "hauntings", and given a series of names linked to the building's history.

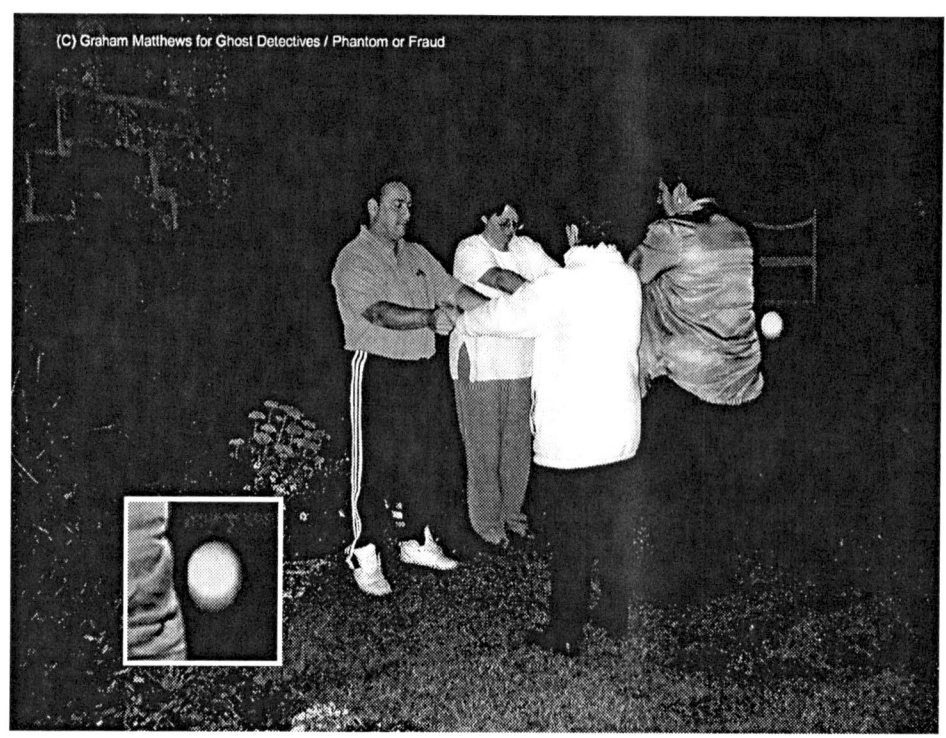

Marion and other sensitives with orb at Dalston Hall.

The evidence captured on photograph and video over five nights, was to say the least, quite compelling, and I could feel myself turning from sceptic, to a far more open-minded investigator, as I realized that some things DEFY rational and logical explanation. I was still a long way from being a firm believer at this stage however.

Two
Ghost Detectives

In the summer of 2001, with a stack of investigations behind us, we suddenly received a phone call from a company called Lion Television who had been commissioned to make 6 one hour shows about "ghosts" for a Halloween special on UK Horizons. Having realized that their own knowledge of the paranormal was inadequate, they had scoured the Internet seeking a group of investigators who would eventually become "The Ghost Detectives".

The original programme submitted had a different working title, but by the time it went to air, the series, fronted by former Dr. Who Tom Baker, was called Ghost Detectives, and the team featured were The Phantom or Fraud Project, including myself, Graham and clairvoyant Marion Goodfellow.

The programme gave us the funding to carry out six 5 night investigations at Bowden House in Devon, Pengersick Castle in Cornwall, The Theatre Royal in Margate, Marsden Grotto in South Shields, Derby Gaol in Derby and The White Hart Hotel in St. Albans.

Lion were worried about how to fill an hour long programme if "no ghosts showed up", and being very skeptical that any actually would, likened it to filming a dinner party with no invited guests. I must admit, that although I boasted that this wouldn't be a problem, I was pulling my own hair out on the subject now that we were under the spotlight, especially after being told by the producer that they may cancel the series if the first investigation did not produce "the goods".

On the first night at an old manor house in Totnes in Devon, the producer arrived having just returned from holiday with only a one hour telephone briefing from Lion, he admitted to being a total sceptic with no real idea how to make a programme about ghosts! As Associate Producer, I sat down with him and together we worked out the best way to get an interesting, informative and watchable programme. Despite my initial worries, he actually turned out to be an excellent choice as Producer for the programme, and far more open-minded than he had earlier admitted. He too, was to undertake a journey over the next few days that he could not have imagined in his wildest dreams!

My dilemma was that he had been told by Lion to "try one episode and if it doesn't work we'll pull the plug after Bowden House". I was faced with the prospect that after all the hard work, it may never actually go to air, and the other five venues may be pulled.

Three days and nights passed with very little evidence of anything remotely associated with the paranormal and day four wasn't looking any better. The team were becoming dismayed and there was a real atmosphere of pessimism in the air.

We held a séance with Marion at the helm, and whilst in trance, she promised "they will dance for us tonight". She channeled what she told us was the ghost of ALICE, a young girl associated with the past of Bowden House who was keen to help us with our work there. Low and behold later that night we were bombarded by three hours of constant "paranormal activity" which to this day has never been rationally explained.

The first thing to happen involved a strange dancing candle flame which appeared to leave the wick, rise several inches above the candle, go out, re-ignite and then move slowly back down to reconnect with the wick. We watched in amazement from the control room on the series of TV monitors set up in front of us. No-one was in the room where the activity had started to happen. We were all baffled.

Then, as if from nowhere, a sudden barrage of floating orbs began dancing around the table in the Great Hall, caught by a small mini-cam with an infrared light source. The orbs appeared to move through the giant table, and three members of the team were sent down to investigate. Upon arrival in the Great Hall, the investigators radioed back to the control room telling of a feeling of extreme static electricity in the room that made the hairs on the backs of their necks stand up. Amongst the team was skeptical author Ruth Stratton who still talks about the incident as a turning point in her own research of the paranormal.

Although the investigators could not SEE the orbs with their own eyes, they could feel the areas where the static levels were high and pointed these out to the watching cameras. This related DIRECTLY to where the orbs were at that time.

The display went on for around three hours with no explanation for what may have caused the phenomena.

Sceptical expert Professor Chris French who did not attend ANY of the investigations in person, was filmed at a later date to analyze the footage claimed by the team to be paranormal, and put the dancing orbs display down to dust in a draught! HOW, if this was the case, did dust only appear one night out of five, in a room with NO apparent draughts. Also, let us not forget that some hours earlier, Marion had said whilst in trance "they will dance for us tonight".

The following day, I had what for me, was a very convincing paranormal encounter. A young girl had been brought in by the Producer to play the part of Alice in a reconstruction in the Pink Room, an area where "Alice's presence" had been reported by various visitors to the building. The girl began skipping around the bed whilst I watched from a quiet corner of the room. Suddenly a voice whispered in my ear "may I play?" I turned around but no-one was there. I froze, and my obvious distressed state was picked up by Graham who alerted the cameramen to start filming ME.

I refused to be filmed about what had happened as I thought I would be made to look mad by the programme. So they turned the cameras off and Graham began to question me in typical police style about what I thought I had heard.

At the end of this intense period of interrogation, Graham pointed out that he had asked me the same questions in various ways, but I had never differed in my explanation of what I had heard "MAY I PLAY". Graham said "are you sure it wasn't "CAN I play", or "Can I join in"? I knew it was MAY I PLAY. Graham then pointed out to the team that this was Victorian Grammar and NOT how a child would speak in 2001. The ghost of Alice was said to be from the Victorian era. Later the same night, another member of the team Andy Matthews (Graham's brother) claimed that Alice appeared to him as a full apparition, although as no one else witnessed this, it could not be used as firm evidence.

With Bowden deemed a success by the Producer, we were now given the green light for the rest of the series.

As the series progressed, it became obvious that we were becoming much closer as a team, and that certain investigators were coming out of themselves, freely admitting that they were willing to talk on camera, something that many did not want to do when the filming began. As the confidence grew, the programme content grew stronger, but retaining the logical and rational approach which was to make Ghost Detectives stand out from other more entertainment based paranormal programmes.

Next stop was Pengersick Castle, in Praa Sands on the Cornish coast. The reputation of being "Britain's most haunted castle" led us to believe we were in for a good week here, but in paranormal research you must never listen to these boasts. I was soon to find out that almost every place I visited claimed to be "the most haunted place in Britain". Very FEW actually produce the evidence to back up such a claim.

The most memorable part of this investigation for me, was another "orb display" on the second night there, but for some reason, this did not look the same to me, and I was certain that this was NOT "spirits at play". The team became excited as more and more "orbs" appeared on the screen, yet only ONE camera in a room with three running, was capturing the anomalies. So I went up to the room to investigate.

After banging cushions trying to recreate dust, searching for draughts and resetting each camera, I noticed that the mini-cam capturing the orbs, was directly behind two large floodlights that had been set up by the TV crew. The lights were throwing beams directly in front of the camera and illuminating the DUST. Yes, on this occasion, we had successfully ruled out paranormal activity, and the disappointed team returned to their experiments.

Pengersick failed to give us any hard evidence of paranormal activity over the five days, but I did learn some valuable new theories on dowsing from a Cornish dowser who works regularly on the site, and I will address these later in this book.

Next stop was the Theatre Royal in Margate, and our first and only meeting with the show's presenter, former Dr. Who, Tom Baker. I found Tom a very strange being, probably from the planet Zwogg, but a true professional when the camera began to run. Tom openly admitted that he did not believe in ghosts, but when asked why, he replied "because they do not believe in me". Hmmmm.

This old theatre was to produce further evidence that was to stun our sceptical TV crew and nearly ended in the death of lead clairvoyant Marion Goodfellow!

Marion had decided to conduct her séance, 60 feet above the stage in the area used by the lighting and props department. Here, high in the rigging, she had earlier picked up on a strong presence that she felt was in desperate need of her help, so we set about running cabling to set up a series of cameras and microphones.

During the séance, she began to channel the alleged spirit of a very frightened man who seemed to become very disturbed by a stage prop of a hangman's noose nearby. She started to shout, it wasn't me, I didn't do it and then lunged towards the edge of the platform where she had been sitting, inches away from a 60 foot sheer drop to the stage. She was saved only by the quick reactions of Graham Matthews and others taking part in the séance who struggled to pull her back. Everyone up there was visibly shocked and they tried for what seemed an eternity, to bring Marion out of trance.

Séance at Margate.

When they returned to the control room, they were all visibly shaken and white as sheets, but it wasn't over yet. Suddenly without warning, another member of the team Pauline Wall, not a clairvoyant, went into what appeared to be a state of trance, and despite attempts to bring her back, she failed to move for several minutes.

Then investigator Guy Deakins looked at me and said "your eyes have changed color, at which point I started to talk with a strange accent, and began to head for the cellar to "show them something they must see". I kept pointing at an area of the cellar beneath the stage, but couldn't make them understand what it was I was attempting to show them, and eventually I collapsed to my knees, and whatever it was had appeared to leave me.

Next to be "hit" was total sceptic Graham Matthews, who suddenly froze bolt upright, his hair standing on end like he had just been plugged into an electric socket. He had stills cameras in both hands which he dropped to the floor (believe me, Graham would NEVER let that happen by choice). He shook violently for several minutes, saying nothing, whilst the clairvoyant team surrounded him trying to clear what they called a "possession". I must admit this was frightening even the strongest amongst us.

Eventually Graham fell to his knees and the activity appeared to stop. Now Graham was one of those people who had always until now, found a rational or logical explanation for such things, and was very much the team sceptic, so we pointed a camera at him and asked him to explain what had just happened. To our surprise he said "sorry guys, you've just lost your sceptic". He then vanished for almost two hours whilst taking a walk along Margate sea front to try to work out in his head what had just happened to him. When he returned, still looking pale and shaky, he admitted that he had NO sensible explanation to offer.

Margate threw up quite a lot of strange phenomena, and I would like to return there one day for some more experiments.

Next stop was Marsden Grotto on the North East coast (yes, anther holiday resort). This building began life as a cave set deep in a cliff face, which was home to its builder Jack "the blaster" Bates. More recently, the building had been used as a wine bar and restaurant, but now stood empty and boarded up.

Again, the venue produced some very strange phenomena, one in particular which thoroughly intrigued me.

Whilst searching through a digital tape for something that had been reportedly seen by an investigator earlier, I came across what appeared to be a shadow walking across a staircase and disappearing through a wall.

This area was lit by an infrared light and covered by a mini-cam at the top of the stairs. The strange thing here, was that the image couldn't be seen in normal play mode, or in any attempt at a freeze frame. The image only appeared in fast forward search/play or fast reverse search/play. This was a physical impossibility, or so we had thought.

We went to the area concerned and made sure that nobody had been walking about in the area at the time of the incident, and concluded that the shadow could NOT have been any of our team or the TV crew.

Now video is shot at a rate of 25 frames per second, and anything outside of this time frame, cannot be of known time-movement. There is a theory however, of what is called TEMPORAL TIME, where movement is outside of our known and accepted time spectrum, only in temporal time, could something appear the way that it did on that day. NOTHING HUMAN that we currently know of, moves in temporal time. The other strange thing about this, was that the shadow appeared to create its OWN shadow which went in the OPPOSITE direction! How can that be?

Another séance was also conducted at the Grotto, and this time we had managed to borrow a thermal imaging camera. Clairvoyants constantly told us that when channeling, they get an immense feeling of cold around their solar plexus, so here was an attempt to prove or disprove that once and for all.

The thermal camera shows heat and cold by color changes on the physical image and therefore any sudden changes in color would denote a change in the clairvoyant's body temperature.

The séance produced very little for about 25 minutes when suddenly Marion whispered, "I have someone here with me". At exactly this moment, the red warm area around the front of her body changed suddenly to blue, indicating sudden coldness. The blue stayed throughout her period in trance, before returning to red at the end. To this day, no-one has managed to give any plausible explanation for what caused this.

Our penultimate programme was made at the underground Gaol in Derby, and here we first met historian Richard Felix, later to become a household name in another paranormal TV series. Richard told us a lot of stories about the old prison, and we eagerly awaited the arrival of the clairvoyant team to see if they could contact any of its ghostly inmates.

It wasn't long before Marion and her clairvoyant colleague Paul Hanrahan, had made contact with a former jailer, also renowned for stalking visitors to the jail, but this was not to be the most intriguing part of this investigation.

I had long been interested in the appearance of orbs in our photographs, and whilst other investigation groups had ceased their research in this area believing them to be only dust, I was not yet convinced that the explanation was quite so straightforward.

So clairvoyant Paul, and investigator Andy Matthews, himself slightly clairvoyant, set up an experiment with me, to see if we could "capture an orb at the point Paul summoned a spirit". Andy was nicknamed "the orb catcher" because of his ability as a sensitive, to take photographs of orbs almost at will, so we gave him the camera and filmed the experiment taking place.

Paul sat on a chair and closed his eyes, apparently "expanding his aura" in an attempt to "draw spirit close". Paul suddenly said "take a picture of me right now, there is someone by my arm" – Andy took a picture, low and behold an orb appeared by Paul's arm. The pair became excited at their evidence, but we pointed out that we must rule out co-incidence. I asked that Andy take a series of shots of the room before we recommenced the experiment. NO ORBS appeared in any of these pictures.

Paul again sat down on the chair and followed the same procedure as before. After a few minutes he said "he is back, he is now standing behind me" – Andy moved quickly around the room and photographed Paul's back, to our total astonishment, an orb appeared in the centre of Paul's back.. The experiment was declared a success, and much excitement was felt throughout the gaol.

We must remember however, that with stills cameras, we produce a 2 dimensional image, and "depth of field" is a major factor in exactly WHERE the orb appeared. Without proof of where the orb actually was, we cannot be certain whether it was a large circle on Paul's back or a tiny anomaly caught out of focus, very close to the lens.

Graham Matthews, who apart from being a Police Officer, was a well respected photographer, was not convinced by this experiment, and felt that co-incidence still played a large part. Unfortunately time had run out on us and we were unable to repeat the experiment.

The final stop on our filming tour of the UK, was in the historic town of St. Albans at the ancient White Hart Hotel.

At Derby, Lion had taken away our producer to make a start on editing the first four programmes, and had brought in a replacement who was not generally liked by my team, and tensions between us and Lion TV had reached boiling point. It seemed that the new producer wanted to use the small amount of what remained as a budget, on reconstructions rather than pay my team members what they had been promised, and to this day I really have no idea how this last show ever got made without a complete mutiny.

Ghost Detective Team at St. Albans.

I was helping the team rig cameras and cabling throughout the building when someone called me on the radio and told me that a camera in one of the two main cellar areas had suddenly been catapulted across the room! Myself and two other team members hurried down to investigate this alleged "poltergeist activity". No-one had been in this cellar at the time, as was verified by other cameras, yet this camera was on the floor several feet away from where I had placed it some time before, with the wires ripped from the back.. The tripod had not just fallen over it had appeared to be projected some distance from where it had been placed, and there were no signs of any animals in the cellar (rats or the like) that could have caused such damage. I later found out that poltergeist activity in this room was well documented by staff and management of the premises.

In the same cellar area a couple of days into the investigation, clairvoyant Marion Goodfellow suddenly became terrified and started to scream at the top of her voice "the ghosts, the ghosts I'm afraid of the ghosts", she began shaking and crying, sobbing and screaming at those around her, saying that she had been shut in there in the dark and was afraid of the ghosts. She then announced herself as Rebecca and started to tell of a fire. It was some considerable time before Marion could be calmed by those around her.

Now whilst nothing appeared on our initial research to back up her story, we sent researchers Suzie Millar and Ruth Stratton out to the local libraries and local government archives to see if we could find any trace of a "Rebecca". Imagine our surprise when Ruth returned saying she had found a Rebecca who had died in a fire whilst trapped in that very cellar where she had been locked in as a punishment by her cruel guardians.

This information came from deep within the archives, and was not accessible from the libraries or via the Internet, so there appears to be no way that the clairvoyant could have known about this incident prior to the investigation. Even the staff and management had no prior knowledge of this particular story.

The footage of Marion was so disturbing, that Lion TV decided not to include it in the programme, to my utter disbelief.

We now waited patiently to watch our six programmes go to air. The programmes went out over Halloween weekend in 2001, and apparently were a major ratings success for the channel.

The phone began to ring, and I found myself taking part in radio programmes all over the world as the man from TV's "Ghost Detectives", with the presenters proudly claiming that their guest was at the very cutting edge of scientific paranormal research. I was very flattered, but at that time still thought of myself as somewhat of a novice.

I was then invited as guest on the Lorraine Kelly TODAY programme on GMTV to discuss the series, and was picked up in the early hours of the morning by a chauffeur in a very posh limousine, only to be returned home after the show in a Skoda.

Despite the excellent ratings, UK Horizons failed to offer a second series, and other paranormal shows were popping up on other channels, pushing us out of the limelight.

From hereon, I realized that to take The Phantom or Fraud Project forward, many changes were needed, if we were to stay at the "cutting edge" of paranormal research, and to fund these changes, we NEEDED television monies.

Three
Affairs, Separations, Divorce & Ghosts!

Being away for long periods of time on investigations, and for filming, was taking a toll on the lives of many of the investigators, and many friendships began to develop into much more intimate affairs whilst things at home were becoming anything but rosy. The Phantom or Fraud Project was becoming more like the Phantom or Fuck Project.

Graham was getting a bit of a reputation with the ladies who had nicknamed him "the gynecologist" and not because of any medical skills he may have possessed. It was at this point that he confided in me that his own marriage was on the rocks and that he was about to leave his wife and move in with a woman he had met through Phantom.

I was not without blemish here either, having become more than a little embroiled with one of our researchers Suzie Millar, whilst filming Ghost Detectives. In late 2002, it became obvious that my own marriage was in severe difficulty, mainly due to myself and my wife wanting entirely different things in life. I finally gave up on the marriage after 18 years together, in January 2003, at which point Graham had just returned to his wife!

Suzie and I had grown a lot closer in the last year of my marriage to Irene, and had even discussed marriage. She was giving me sexually and personally what I had lacked for so many years in my marriage, and wrong though I knew it was, I felt that my marriage to Irene had been dead more than two years before I left her but had stayed for the sake of my three beautiful daughters Leanne, Amanda and Nikki.

Suzie and I had taken every opportunity to be together on investigations, and she gave me the love, affection and cuddles that were missing at home. She was a very affectionate person and also extremely protective of me when we were out working. She was also an inspiration to me spiritually, although I didn't realize that until a lot later.

Things were at a low ebb, my ex had all the savings, my house, my kids and all the furniture, Although the parting was not because of any other person being involved at that time, she was still very bitter that I had walked out, and what was to become a two year court battle for access and money, began. She still knew nothing about Suzie and I at this time.

Around the same time, Graham and I were continually arguing about the way Phantom should be run, which would lead to us parting company and going our own ways. I was deeply saddened that this had happened, I had always thought of Graham as a true friend and drinking partner. These were indeed sad times in my life. But I was determined to keep Phantom running and began the long battle to rebuild the Project. Little did I know how these changes, were to take me head long into the world of SCIENCE, a radio show, but further away from television.

When I walked out on my family, I moved in for a short period with Suzie, but it very quickly became apparent that it was never going to work. Her interests and mine were very different, and I didn't believe she was the sort of person who could be tied down to a long term relationship, and decided to end things and move into a place on my own. I was left looking for a cheap flat on the poor side of town.

The effects of the growing bitterness between myself and my ex-wife had now began to take it's toll and I was missing Suzie more than I could ever have imagined and in the spring of 2003, I came the closest I had ever been to meeting our spirit friends head-on…I was contemplating suicide.

They say that real friends are the ones that are really there when you need them, and whilst I sat in my office on a rainy Sunday afternoon contemplating how I would do it, the phone rung, and one of my investigators Helen Livesey-Jones was on the other end. "I knew you were there" she said "and I know something is wrong, and I want you to come and stay with us in Chepstow for a while".

Despite my denials, and assurances that I was fine, Helen could always read me like a book, and finally I broke down in tears as I told her how I was feeling. She persuaded me to take the two hour drive from Dunstable to Chepstow, where I stayed for almost three weeks. I honestly believe that if she hadn't made that call, I may be writing this book via automatic writing with the aide of a psychic medium.

Suzie and I had stayed at Helen and Mike's on a number of occasions and it felt very strange to be in that double bed alone. For a time the depression grew deeper,

Helen and her partner Mike Cannaby spent the next few weeks getting me back on track, and slowly I started to rebuild my life. I had spent days doing nothing but playing Championship Manager, a football strategy game I had become addicted to, and moping around their house to and from their PC hoping there may be some good news in my e-mail inbox.

Mike's sister Sue, was also a clairvoyant and whilst at their house, showed me that I too had some of these "talents" and began to teach me how to use my own senses in a way that I had never before thought possible.

It was at Chepstow, whilst talking to Sue, Helen and Mike, that I realized the importance of PROVING the existence of life after death, and thus it became a new chapter in my quest for the truth. Slowly and surely I began to rebuild my life.

I eventually returned to Dunstable and found myself a flat and invited my eldest daughter Leanne to come live with me, as she had been diagnosed with ADHD (Attention Deficit Hyperactive Disorder) and her Mum had all three kids to cope with, so I thought I may be able to take some of the stress and try to help.

Some months passed by, and whilst I was still under enormous financial pressure, I was starting to look towards the future and began socializing again.

Before Graham had left Phantom, we had taken a stall at the Fortean Times exhibition in London UNCONVENTION 2003, and we offered the visitors the opportunity to meet the team from Ghost Detectives and join us as investigators on the Project.

Amongst the new faces joining up was Devon based divorcee Penny Dando, whom I felt myself being attracted to! Little did I know that just a few months later, I would be engaged to her, and she would be taking over Graham's position as my partner in the Phantom or Fraud Project.

Penny attended one of the paranormal training courses that Graham and I had launched in 2003, and it was here that the relationship began. I have to say looking back, that Penny was the most important person ever to enter my life. At a time where my life had little direction and seemingly little purpose, she gave that life the meaning.

I heard that after Penny joined Phantom or Fraud that she was to attend an investigation at the Barnfield Theatre in Exeter with team leader Mark Norman, so I contacted Mark and said that I would be coming down to join him on the stake-out. He was a little surprised that I was willing to travel 200 miles for a one night investigation, but I think he knew my REAL motives.

At the investigation, I used every opportunity I could to get close to Penny even holding her hand in a "séance" in the theatre seating area. Then whilst climbing the stairs to an upstairs gallery area I said "you have amazing eyes". The way she looked at me made me think "oh shit I've blown it" but I later learned that it was just her surprise at me being quite so forward!

Penny told me some time later that she had quizzed the other girls on the investigation about my comments thinking that maybe I say that to all the girls, but was told that was not the case!

It was after the investigation that things started to build at speed, during a series of nightly MSN conversations on the Internet, and then phone calls, where it became obvious that she felt the same way about me as I felt about her. A sexual chemistry was building that was to explode on our next meeting.

Penny came up to Dunstable for our training course, and we kissed passionately for the first time upon her arrival. Throughout the training course others became aware of the eye contact between us, and when the course broke off for an evening meal, Penny and I went off to a local restaurant where it became obvious that we were falling in love.

Later that night she chose not to stay at the hotel room she had booked, but returned to my flat with me, where we were literally ripping off each others clothes on the stairs as we entered!

Each weekend after that Penny would make the 400 mile round trip to be with me in Dunstable, and after several moths asked me to move to Exeter with her, which I did.

Since Penny and I have been together, times have been very difficult, both with the divorce from Irene, constant court battles over money and my children, and an on-going run of financial misfortune, but unlike any other I had loved before, she was always there with a kiss, a cuddle and the love and warmth that one needs to much when times are bad.

As she helped me to rebuild Phantom or Fraud, Penny became not only my partner, my lover, my friend and my confidant, but also a business partner and mentor. In December 2003 at the annual Phantom or Fraud Christmas party, I got down on one knee in front of everyone and asked her to marry me.

I look back and consider myself so fortunate to have found a true soul-mate, someone I honestly believe I will spend the rest of my life with, someone who at last I can truly say, I really love.

Our training courses were great fun, they involved teaching amateur ghost-hunters and those who had never tried it before, how to run a professional and scientific stake-out of a haunted location, covering cameras, video techniques, working with clairvoyants, insurance implications and general event management. After the five hour course, the trainees would be taken on a REAL paranormal investigation of an alleged haunted location nearby. Many of those attending went on to form their own paranormal organizations, such as Heidi Graham from UK Ghost Investigators. The courses also provided the much needed income to fund our research.

Penny had encouraged me to get back on paranormal investigations and take The Phantom or Fraud Project to new heights. After a very quiet spell, the Ghost Detective was ready to return!

Four
Other Reasons for Paranormal Activity?

Until now, we have looked at "paranormal activity" as being either rationally explained, or being the work of those who have departed this life, but could there be OTHER reasons that may explain some or all of this strange phenomena?

The first area we must look at is CAUSE and EFFECT – and by this I mean, is what we see, photograph, film, the CAUSE of the activity, or an effect of such activity happening?

As an example, let us look at ORBS, which many still believe to be no more than dust….

If a room is still and quiet and has been left this way under monitored camera conditions for several days, and no draughts or major sources of airflow have been encountered, then what could these orbs be?

If the orb IS, as we have investigated, the energy/soul form, then we would need real evidence to substantiate such a bold claim. But imagine if the real activity could NOT be seen or filmed, but in its very actions, STIRRED UP the dust in the room, then orbs would be an EFFECT rather than the cause.

Let us also look at the "full body apparition". If, when we die, our bodies are buried or cremated, then why should we return looking the same way? If only our consciousness or energy survives, we would probably take on a form similar to that of electricity, and thus invisible to the human eye. How then, do people see this "apparition", is it their own imagination, or perhaps a transmitted telepathy from the consciousness direct to the viewer?

Another theory, is that some ghost sightings, may be like 3D video replays of the past, where the apparition is seen in the same place over and over again doing exactly the same thing, and appears not to react to things and people around it. If there was a sudden massive explosion of emotion such as a sudden death, murder or suicide, maybe this is recorded by Quartz Crystal in the very walls of the building, and replayed through time?

Imagine also, that there are parallel dimensions alongside of our very own, perhaps every now and then, someone slips through the gauze between these dimensions and appears out of focus or alignment and thus "ghostly" in their appearance?

One notable case in our early investigations, involved medium Marion Goodfellow seeing a "maid" apparently cleaning a chandelier in the MOD's Chicksands Priory. She was going about her everyday tasks and was quite surprised when Marion asked her when she had "passed". Marion said she replied "I am not dead, is it perhaps YOU that is?" Do we therefore appear as ghosts to them in their dimension?

On another investigation at the Lilley Arms in Hertfordshire, the landlady told us that she confronted an apparition in the lounge bar of the pub, and asked what he was doing in her home, she was amazed when he replied to her "I think madam that it is YOU who is in MY home". Could he really have believed that SHE was the intruder?

The parallel dimension theory is a fairly sound one, and many scientists now believe that we may form part of a multi-dimensional universe.

I will look deeper at the parallel dimension theory later in this book.

Another theory that covers many night-time apparitions, is that of the sleep deprivation and sleep paralysis, which causes what seems at the time to be a very real paranormal experience. Reports often follow a very similar line…

The person experiencing the event reports waking up suddenly and often sitting bolt-upright, seeing someone standing at the end of the bed, or a feeling of someone pressing down on them or holding them down forcibly. Many of these reports involve an "old hag" a haggard looking old woman, and the description of this woman is always very similar in these reports.

Another area worth studying, is that of geographic fault lines. These natural energy centers of the Earth itself, have often been said to generate small glowing lights and "ball lightning" often reported as UFO's, and in an edition of William Woollard's Ghosthunters programme, he found evidence to support the claim that many paranormal encounters are on or very close to, geographic fault lines.

If geographic fault lines are a CAUSE of what appears as paranormal activity, then much more research is required in this area to provide real evidence to substantiate such a claim.

One of MY theories however, is that Earth energies, such as those allegedly generated by these fault lines, MAY actually energise the soul/spirit form, or a vortex gateway, thus powering the paranormal activity and allowing them to manifest. Again, there is little real evidence to support this theory as yet.

With new technology being brought onto the market everyday, I honestly believe that if we had the financial resources available to purchase these items at will, we would be much further forward in our research.

Five
My First Meeting with Dr. Sam Parnia

Dr. Sam Parnia works as a Doctor at Southampton General Hospital, and when we first met in 2002, he had just finished working on an in-depth study of near-death experiences.

Parnia and I had been in contact by e-mail for some period prior to our meeting, and he had shown a great interest in the work of The Phantom or Fraud Project, as he had recognized likenesses between some of our study results, and his own.

At the time, I had just appointed a series of investigators as "team leaders" to control investigations in various areas of the country, and to take some of the pressure to arrange stake-outs, off the shoulders of Graham and I. To assist with this, I promoted investigator Norie Miles from Portsmouth, to the position of National Co-Coordinator to oversee the team leaders, thus creating a management line structure to the organization.

I arranged a meeting with Dr. Parnia at the hospital, and as I also had to meet with Norie, I decided to kill two birds with one stone, and fit both appointments into the same trip. Norie then told me SHE would love to sit in on the meeting with Parnia, so accompanied me to Southampton.

Now I have to admit to not being the greatest fan of hospitals, I always find them to have a certain smell that causes me to want to make the swiftest of exits. So having to sit in a waiting area whilst they located and called Dr. Parnia, made me feel like I was about to undergo a Rossiotomy.

When Dr. Parnia finally appeared, he looked very different to how I imagined him. It is strange how we start to visualize people before we have met them, and just how wrong we can be. He led us to a restaurant area, ordered some hot drinks and sat down with Norie and I to discuss the issues in hand.

It seems that he started out, like most of us, as a sceptic. Looking into the old theories of chemicals within the brain, such as Melatonin and Serotonin, causing hallucinations at the point of bodily death, but like me, he had been puzzled as to how everyone reported a very similar experience. If you put 10 people in a room and gave them all a hallucinatory drug such as LSD (not recommended by author!) they would all have VERY different hallucinations. So why should Serotonin and the like, give all NDE's the same experience?

Parnia had looked into many cases, where patients had "died" whilst in the operating theatre, usually through cardiac arrest or similar events. Whilst clinically brain-dead, Parnia had believed it would not be possible for them to relate any direct experience. His research was to prove him wrong.

Most of the patients he interviewed that had been through a near-death experience, reported astonishingly similar events. Firstly, they appear to have a sensation of leaving their physical body, and floating above the operating table, at which time they can "see" and "hear" what is happening around them in the theatre. They can often report conversations being had by the medical team, machines being wheeled in or out of the theatre, and can see the resuscitation team at work.

More strangely perhaps, they see a ball or tunnel of light appearing to move towards them, which then seems to transfigure into a bodily apparition familiar to them, such as a dead relative or friend who then tells them that it is not yet their time.

Now let's break down Parnia's comments here, and compare it to our work as paranormal investigators....

Firstly, if they have LEFT their physical bodies, how do they "see" or "hear", as they would now be in "energy or consciousness form" and would have no eyes or ears? Perhaps we can bring TELEPATHY/ESP into our thoughts at this point to help us understand a possible explanation?

On paranormal investigations, we admit to photographing the "orb" (a ball or tunnel of light), yet the clairvoyant/mediums tell us they see the physical bodily apparition. Could it be that the orb is in fact the energy/consciousness retaining personality, and creating a physical picture by telepathy/ESP for the clairvoyant to see? Perhaps they can project an image of how they looked in their human life form? This would also explain why in a room full of people, only one person ever claims to see the full body apparition, as telepathy appears to be a one-to-one experience.

Now Parnia was intrigued by this theory, and at this point, admitted for the first time that he now believes that a "consciousness" or "soul" may well survive human bodily death, albeit maybe only momentarily. When we questioned him on an "after-life" he replied "well that's your research, mine stops at the NDE's for now". I think as a Doctor, he could not afford to be seen associating himself publicly with paranormal research, as it may be detrimental to his professional standing. When oh WHEN are science and medicine going to realize that our research IS a scientific area, and not the work of the mind. That said, I have to say that there ARE now many scholars, scientists and doctors, who ARE recognizing the importance of our work, and of properly examining the paranormal.

Let us not forget, that the word "paranormal" purely covers that which cannot currently be described as "normal". Electricity may well have been deemed paranormal once, until science explained it to the masses.

At this point, the extremely tired Norie had dozed off and was snoring quietly at the corner of the table – I guess she had heard me state my personal theories, once too often. Parnia looked at her, then back at me and smiled.

I then showed him some orb pictures, and he was fascinated at the similarity between these, and what his patients had described in their reports as the "ball or tunnel" of light.

Parnia was keen for me to promote his work, as he needed like ourselves, to attract considerable funding to take his research further forward and to carry out longer and deeper studies of this strange phenomena.

I spoke to him about the work of Dr. MacDougall in Massachusetts in the early 1900's, and he was very aware of his experiments. MacDougall had set up a bed in a hospital, on scales, and weighed people in their dying moments. Each apparently had an unexplained weight loss within minutes of their death which was NOT down to exhalation, bodily fluid release, or other events known at the point of passing. He put this down to what he believed was a "spirit or soul" leaving the body.

Now if we think logically, and our body is run by an energy source, energy is a "mass" and mass has weight, so MacDougall's theory certainly has substance. To my knowledge, no-one has repeated these experiments as yet, with the new technology available to us today.

Now as an example, think of this energy in relation to that of a car…. If your car has "died" perhaps wrecked in an accident, it will go to a scrap yard and be squashed into a 3 foot cube. But before this happens, they may take out the engine (the energy source) which is still working and sell it to someone else. So your car's "energy" may still be "alive" and driving up and down the motorway daily, but unrecognizable to you in it's new "body". Could this be related to the human reincarnation theory perhaps?

Parnia was fascinated by our research, and requested that we stay in close contact, comparing notes on our particular fields of research.

I woke a somewhat embarrassed Norie up, and we thanked Dr. Parnia for his time, and left on our way back to her home in Portsmouth. Even though she had missed a large amount of what was discussed, she had heard enough to believe that we were getting closer to finding the truth.

The quest for further evidence of soul survival continued.

Six
The Colchester Incident

Let's go back to an investigation that happened whilst I was still married…

I remember Colchester for two reasons – the first a paranormal investigation at the Black Swan pub, and the second my first real encounter as a "psychic" in a spiritualist church.

We were approached by a landlord of a public house in Stanway near Colchester who said that he was experiencing strange poltergeist style activity, and with my desire to encounter a poltergeist head-on, I quickly arranged the investigation and we set off to find out what was happening.

Upon arrival I was briefed on some of the problems which included a chair moving on its own, electrical appliances that would switch themselves on and off even when "UNPLUGGED" and a flood that seemed to come through the ceiling above the bar, yet when inspected, the ceiling wasn't even DAMP! I must admit to being somewhat excited at the thought of spending some time here.

We carried out some initial tests with EMF meters and dowsed the premises from top to bottom, then set about the arduous task of rigging cables up and down stairs throughout the bars and installing the cameras.

Over the course of two days and nights we did indeed witness some very strange phenomena, although some of it was to become even stranger in the future.

I was working with two investigators in one upstairs room in the pub, and was dowsing what I believed to be a "portal". This is an area of energy where we believe that spirit may enter and leave our dimension.

Marion Goodfellow entered the room and immediately picked up on something close to where I was standing, but made the strange comment "there is someone here but it is not a spirit." One of the investigators Joy Henson then said "I can hear a man's voice" which shook me as I had heard it too but had not said anything. Once you start admitting you are hearing voices, I believed it was time to go off to the funny farm.

The voice then announced he was from our future and began to tell us of a "war that would start in America" he also indicated explosions and tall buildings on fire. We had no idea at that time of what was to happen in the now well documented 9/11 attacks. He also foretold of tsunamis, storms and earthquakes all of which have since come to be. Still to this very day I cannot believe that we were told all of this information but did nothing, believing it impossible!

We talked at length between ourselves about the incident after it had happened and decided that to announce this at the time, would make fools of us all if it didn't happen, so we stayed quiet. After all, if you heard voices in your ear telling you that he was from your future, what would you have done?

Later in the same investigation, we witnessed a dish-washer in the bar area turning itself on and off, and despite a series of electrical tests there appeared to be no visible fault in the machine or the supply. Again, around the machine was a feeling of high-energy and static, and other nearby electrical appliances also began to fail. At the same time, batteries in our video cameras were suddenly emptied for no apparent reason. We could find no explanation for this strange course of events.

The landlord and his partner were transferred to another pub shortly after this investigation, and when we checked with the new management team, they reported absolutely NO paranormal activity at the Black Swan. Could it be the case that PEOPLE rather than PLACES set off this activity, or attract the paranormal?

On a separate visit to Colchester a year or so later, I accompanied Suzie Millar to a spiritualist church where she wanted me to meet a clairvoyant medium doing a demonstration there. His name was "Brig". But from the moment I took my seat, I found myself intrigued by a woman sitting at the back of the small church, behind me. She must have been conscious of the fact I kept turning and looking at her, but I had no idea why I was doing this.

I turned to Suzie and whispered to her what I was feeling and she said "it happens in these places just go with your gut feelings, don't hold back". She squeezed my hand, smiled and carried on watching the events at the front of the church. I Tried to push it to the back of my mind, as I was feeling quite uncomfortable and fidgety by now.

Brig took to the stage and begun his demonstration of clairvoyance, but still my mind was on the lady at the back.

When he had finished Suzie beckoned me to go to the front to meet him, but my senses were still telling me there was more important business to be done at the back of the church, and whatever was with me that night was becoming impatient and started to push me round to face this woman who by now was putting on her coast ready to leave. I suddenly found myself walking away from Brig and Suzie and heading swiftly towards the exit, still not knowing why or what I was going to say! I was in a sate of panic.

I reached out to the woman and put my hand on her shoulder and suddenly without warning told her that her best friend had recently passed away, described her, told the woman what she died of, and said "you were about to go abroad together, she says you are thinking of cancelling now that she has gone, you must not, she says you MUST STILL GO". At this point I suddenly noticed tears streaming from her eyes, she hugged me and said "my darling I have no idea who you are, but thank you so very much. If my husband was here now he would shake your hand".

It appears the information, name and cause of death I gave her was 100% accurate and that she had been in turmoil since her friend's death, not knowing whether to continue her trip to Egypt or if to cancel it. Her husband had said she must still go it was what her friend would have wanted. To this day, I have no idea where this information came from and how I could have known it, or delivered it to a complete stranger.

Suzie looked at me smiled, kissed me gently on the cheek and whispered "it's just the beginning Ross, you have the gift of the knowing". I was speechless.

Seven
The Tower of London Live!

At the time of writing this book, I believe that the Phantom or Fraud Project is STILL the only paranormal research organization ever to be allowed to spend two nights on a stake-out in the building they call the most haunted place in the world, the Tower of London.

It was 2001 and the Ghost Detectives series was edited and ready to air, when we were approached by a Producer from BBC Worldwide who said he was planning a live TV show form the Tower of London and wanted the "Ghost Detectives" to be there – an offer that I could not possibly turn down!

The first meeting took place between Andrew Sewell, from BBC Worldwide, myself, Andy Mathews from my team and an associate of Mr. Sewell's from the BBC at a pub just up the road from the BBC's offices. The first thing Mr. Sewell wanted to know was whether we were "serious" about paranormal investigation, or just fooling around with ghost-hunting. After spending some 20 minutes convincing him of just how serious we were, my mobile phone went off playing my then ringtone of the Theme from Ghostbusters". There was a moment of silence as Andy Matthews looked at me and bit his lip – then everyone burst out laughing and Mr. Sewell said "OK you're in".

The Tower of London show was a one hour live TV broadcast for UK Horizons, to follow the Ghost Detectives series, but was a two night live web broadcast via the

Internet, the first such venture to be attempted and a forerunner for later shows like Most Haunted Live.

When we arrived at the Thistle Hotel where the BBC had booked us to stay, there was already an air of excitement, but there were some very disgruntled and unhappy members of the team that were not able to come due to the limit of the team size put on us by the BBC and that had taken a toll on the rest of us, we knew it would cause problems at a later date.

I had to share a room with Andy Matthews and it was here that my reputation of being "one of the world's loudest snorers" began!

We slept for a few hours (well at least I did) before setting off for a night in the Tower. We were issued with our passes and ventured onto the television set which had been erected on Tower Green. The presenters were two of the original cast of Blakes 7, namely Claudia Christian and Paul Darrow. As the show went to air, talkback failed and the presenters stared blankly at the screens. Andy and I looked at each other and thought – well it can only get better from here.

As we started our investigation it became obvious that the walkway by the Bloody Tower and the stairs down seemed to be the most active for paranormal activity and it was here that Graham captured what he believed to be his best orb picture ever.

Andy walked down the stairs from the walkway and Graham was at the foot of the same stairway, Graham said "my God I feel like something has just walked right through me, Andy suddenly said she has she is now here right in front of me, Graham took a picture and low and behold there was an orb directly within Andy's eye line to his chest. Graham believes to this day that this ruled out any depth of field discrepancies and as they both felt the spirit, this orb HAD to be of paranormal origin.

A couple of hours later I was filming outside the entrance to the room at the top of the Bloody Tower when an orb crossed the corridor in front of me and was clearly visible on the tape. It was immediately played back to the audience by now watching online on the Internet, with excited acclaim by the presenters.

Ruth Stratton and I also witnessed some strange activity in the Beauchamp Tower with an orb seemingly disappearing through a doorway after crossing the floor in front our very eyes. We also heard strange moaning noises within the room whilst sitting there in pitch darkness.

Andy Matthews with an orb in the Tower of London.

On the second night the word went round that Sir Cliff Richard was getting a private tour, imagine my team's surprise when Cliff and I struck up a conversation about the show. I had met Cliff before and always liked him, but I'm not sure that his Christian beliefs give him a real understanding of the paranormal.

As the investigation drew to a close, we were happy that we had documented a lot of potential paranormal activity for the TV programme, but as for it being the most haunted place in the world, I'll reserve my judgement for now.

Eight
The New Jersey Vortex

Strange phenomena is not restricted to any one place. So when we were invited to check out an alleged "vortex" in Wannaque, New Jersey in January 2002, I was keen to take a team out to check it out.

A vortex has many meanings depending on who is talking to you, but in this case, Bryan Williams, AKA "Sargel 18", believed it to be a doorway to another dimension where strange phenomena is witnessed on an almost daily basis. A claim far too good to miss out on.

I chose my team based on experience and talents and set off for the USA with a view to making a TV programme of this character Sargel 18 and his Vortex. He renamed himself Sargel 18 based upon his 18 reincarnations he believed he had in the past, the present and the future yet to come. He made some very bold claims about his own abilities, his contacts with aliens and having stepped through this dimensional doorway on one or more occasions – so I was sure that either way it would make a great TV documentary.

Upon arrival there was an immediate argument with Sargel about TV rights and monies, which always makes you wonder what people are REALLY in it for, but having sorted the problems, we eventually set out for the vortex on our second night in the area.

It was indeed a very strange place made all the spookier by the trees and animal noises in the woodland area. It apparently was once the site of a munitions factory and stories abounded of an explosion in the 1920's that may have ripped a hole in the space-time continuum although our research showed no evidence of such an explosion. The land opposite was owned by the international company DuPont, and Sargel was convinced that they were linked in some way to government conspiracies and a secret UFO landing site – although again there was no evidence to back up any of these claims.

We did catch some very strange things on camera and film whilst there, although much of this was breath from the camera operators in the below freezing conditions. However Sargel stated that the breath only illuminated what the eye couldn't see under normal conditions, and certainly some photographs did appear to have some strange shapes. Because of copyright wrangles, Sargel would not allow us to show you these photos in this book, however some remain on his web site which you can find by searching Sargel 18 on one of the Internet search engines.

One photo appears to show a hunter holding a spear, and another seems to clearly show a woman in a white dress with no legs or feet floating in the air.

In another picture Sargel showed us, there is a creature apparently floating some 20 feet in the air and bearing an uncanny resemblance to the Loch Ness Monster. Sargel said he showed this picture to a paleobotanist who confirmed it as a prehistoric dinosaur of some kind. He explained "perhaps in our dimension it is 20 feet in the air, but in it's own dimension it could be swimming in water". Could this provide new food for thought for what appears to be in Loch Ness too?

The energies at the home of Sargel and at the vortex, were promoted as being very negative by our host and his girlfriend Sandra, and it had such a devastating effect on Joy, James and Guy, that none of them came with us to the vortex on the first night, and in fact Guy left Sargel's home and went missing in the woods for several hours before walking some 5 miles back to the motel where we were based.

Marion, our clairvoyant, said that negativity breeds negativity and said that being a positive person herself all she saw was light and angels. It was interesting that on entering the "vortex" in Wannaque, we passed a number of homes sporting upside down pentacles and other witchcraft symbols in their windows.

We visited the area constantly over the space of 10 days sometimes at night and sometimes during the day, and we did notice on two occasions that we were being watched by a man in black with a blacked out crash helmet on a tracker bike. It may have just been a local person out having fun, but this was followed by a sudden large amount of traffic to my web site by US GOVERNMENT and US MILITARY servers, the day after I did a live radio interview on the Jeff Rense Show from Sargel's home in New Jersey.

I certainly didn't see anything that convinced me that it was a doorway between dimensions, but I remain intrigued by some of the very strange photographs taken there.

Whilst there, we met up with clairvoyant Cathe Curtis and her partner (photographer Rick Fulton) who at the time lived in Bucks County PA, and they invited us to spend the last couple of days of our trip at their home where Cathe would introduce us to "Henry" her resident ghost.

Imagine 7 or 8 of us asleep on the lounge floor of this small flat – bodies strewn from every angle and enough snoring to wake the dead!

Cathe had been introduced to us as a very powerful medium and clairvoyant and even Marion our own psychic was surprised at the talent of this lady. She summoned spirits to appear for the camera constantly over the two days we were there and on our last day, she summoned one over the heads of each of my team, and sure enough there were the orbs in the photographs!

I had come to the conclusion by this time, that some people have a natural gift to be able to bridge the gap between us and the other side whether it be "the dead talking" or just an ESP/telepathy of some kind. Maybe they are even able to project their own energy as "orbs" – but one way or another – there are a few gifted people with exceptional psychic skills.

Nine
Working with Other Paranormal Organizations

I have never known an area like the paranormal, for so many people doing the same research yet not sharing their experiences with other groups. It seems like every paranormal group wants to be the first to prove the existence of life after death, and refuse outright to work alongside others for the mutual common goal.

Phantom or Fraud has been attacked by numerous other organizations simply because we do go out and promote our work on radio, TV and in the press, and jealous fellow investigators have criticized me in forums for "self-promotion" when all I am doing is promoting my work and research, it's not like I've ever made any money from paranormal research, in fact its cost me thousands.

I used to speak regularly on the telephone with Montage Keen from the SPR (Society for Psychical Research) who passed away a short time ago (although he has kept in contact from the other side, not only with us, but with mediums around the world). Monty was a great thinker and a good reliable scientific investigator of anomalous phenomena. He took part in the Scole Experiment and in physical mediumship circles with David Thompson. In fact in the end, Monty became convinced that these circles did produce phenomena which would indicate the existence of an afterlife.

I also keep in close touch with Maurice Gross, whose remarkable work in poltergeist phenomena, including the Enfield Poltergeist incident, has made him a leading light in the field.

In general however, very few other organizations share their research with us or others and I feel now is the time to try to bring some of these leading organizations like The Ghost Club, CSICOP, ASSAP and the SPR together working as one, and then maybe research would move forward at a faster rate.

I must also point out that there are many organizations purporting to carry out "scientific paranormal research" but on deeper examination are either money making ventures for the group's owners or self-promotional vehicles for failed actors and the like! If you are thinking of joining a group – be careful to examine their motives, beliefs and goals first. If they are selling chocolate ghosts etc. on their websites, they probably aren't in it to prove soul survival.

One good way to find your feet in the paranormal research field is to go on a haunted weekend break with a recognized tour operator such as Haunting Breaks (www.hauntingbreaks.co.uk) here you can see what sort of experiments are carried out, and be guided through the processes under the watchful eyes of trained team leaders and guides.

One particular success story is that of the UKGI (United Kingdom Ghost Investigators) led by Heidi Graham whom I trained on one of the Phantom or Fraud training courses. She now has over 1000 members and carries out investigations throughout the UK on a very regular basis.

Back in 2002, we carried out an investigation with a now defunct team of investigators from Wiltshire, at The Red Lion which sits within Avebury stone circle. It was our first real experience of a joint investigation, and was well organized and thoroughly enjoyable. It was on this investigation that I launched a new era of orb research.

Through ongoing experiments, we had learned that orbs appear to be sensitive to light, and if you sit quietly in a room for say an hour and then all take pictures with flash cameras at the same time on a count, then an orb will 9 times out of 10 be caught on video leaving the room!

In a room at the Red Lion we tried this over and over again, with someone positioned outside the room with a video camera, and on almost every occasion an orb appeared from the door as if leaving the room as the flashes were fired off inside. If this is DUST then let's set up a church and worship intelligent dust.

The Red Lion also produced some very interesting EVP's (electro-voice phenomena). At the time, our head of sound research was Mike Rogers and he conducted various experiments in a number of rooms at the venue, and captured a number of alleged "voices of the dead". Two clearly say what appears to be names, although neither could be linked with people historically associated with the pub.

The stone circle itself provided me with further evidence of strange unexplainable phenomena, when I joined a clairvoyant circle at midnight out amongst the stones. I started to see strange shapes appearing around me which looked like people wearing hooded cloaks, I then started to talk in what appeared to be a "native American type voice". It appears I was in trance for the very first time.

Above our heads whilst the circle took place, was the most incredible display of meteors or shooting stars I have ever seen.

Shortly after the circle was ended, myself and Norie Miles saw a blue swirling mist appearing in front of us, but as we walked towards it, it seemed to move back staying at the same distance form us throughout the encounter. Norie captured the mist on her digital camera. I have no explanation to offer for what this was or for its strange movement.

As the sun rose over the stone circle it was an awesome sight to behold, and there seemed to be an ever-present tingling energy that to me, was far more powerful than anything I had ever encountered at Stonehenge. I knew I would return regularly to Avebury.

Whilst the Red Lion provided us with a good investigation, Avebury had opened my eyes to phenomena existing way beyond just "ghost-hunting".

Ten
Light & Sound Frequency Phenomena

In 2002, I met Helen Livesey Jones and her partner Mike Cannaby, who were to become great and close friends of mine and eventually even "save my life" as I explained in an earlier chapter. Both seemed to possess sensitivity and clairvoyance skills, but Mike was a computer engineer and had been studying frequencies. Now this fascinated me, as I had believed for some time, that sound and light frequencies may provide us with some answers as to what triggers or happens during alleged paranormal activity.

Mike and I set up a series of experiments with sound frequencies to see what would happen if investigators were subjected to various different audible and non-audible sounds during an investigation.

Dr. Vic Tandy from the University of Coventry had been doing similar experiments at the time, as he believed that certain frequencies triggered the brain into thinking we see something move out of the corner of our eyes.

We played with various frequencies at different levels of volume, above and below the 20 Hz area. It is alleged that we cannot generally hear or make sounds as a human being below 20 Hz. NO experiences were monitored by any investigator taking part, other than a couple reporting feeling sick around 15/16 Hz.

However these are on-going tests and with different people in different places, at varying volumes, the results may change.

Light frequencies are also very important to our research. We were lent a camera kit that was called BVS equipment (Beyond the Visible Spectrum) and used what the inventor Roger Allsopp called "black light". This was a different frequency of infrared (IR), and we used it alongside normal IR cameras.

The normal IR cameras capture orbs frequently, however we have YET to see an orb on the BVS cameras. Could it be that orbs can only be seen under certain frequencies of light, or is it that they are just a freak of the light and that the new equipment is too high quality to see these anomalies?

Other areas of light investigation include using ultra-violet to see what may occur in a room during an investigation using only this light and a range of different cameras.

Many researchers believe that geographic fault lines produce a frequency of sound or a vibration that relates to areas where paranormal activity occurs. My own dowsing seems to indicate there is a difference between LEY lines and natural EARTH ENERGY lines, and I can put down a ley line and take it back up again, but I cannot do this with an energy line.

Another area of frequency research that I find fascinating is that of mediums and general mediumship. It would appear that these clairvoyants tune their bodies when working to a different frequency using their own subconscious. They often go into a trance state and admit to changing their own vibrational level.

If you have ever worked with a team of clairvoyants you may find they all channel different things in the same house or room. The skeptics would argue that this is because it is all fake or that clairvoyance doesn't work, but after years of research I would argue that this is NOT the case at all. I put forward that each clairvoyant medium tunes to a different frequency, and therefore 4 people working in the same room may all tune to different time periods or dimensions.

Imagine this like tuning your radio receiver, if you put four people in a room each with a radio and ask them to tune to their favorite radio station, you will probably get at least THREE different stations playing, depending on the frequency to which each tune their own receiver.

My own research indicates that when you are using tried and tested mediums, all four may produce different results yet all four may well be proven correct when you research the building's history!

So how do we further our research into frequencies? It is my intention to get science to help in this respect. If a university can set up a series of experiments with mediums, using different frequency ranges, and monitor each participant when channeling, I believe we may learn more about how these apparently gifted people can change their own bodily frequency.

Eleven
Telepathy & ESP

Telepathy and ESP (Extra-Sensory Perception) is an area that has long fascinated me, and deals with methods of communication between people without the use of speech, and the ability to apparently know things before you have been told about their occurrence.

Have you ever gone to pick up the telephone before it starts ringing, or said to someone "I feel that something has happened to my mother/father"? If you have and you have been correct, chances are you have experienced ESP.

When someone has a near-death experience (NDE) I believe they are also experiencing ESP or telepathy. Think about this for a minute or two…..The person "dies" on the operating table and relates the events that took place during the period of "death". They usually first experience floating above their body and looking down at themselves below, together with the medical team. They then say that they see a bright light or tunnel of light which then manifests into a friend or relative that they recognise who then speaks to them.

Now if they are above their body, they are in energy form, they have left the human body behind, so they have no eyes – so how do they SEE this tunnel of light? They also have no ears – so how do they HEAR the image speaking to them? Surely the ONLY possible answer is telepathy?

If indeed their experience is real, then the vision they are seeing and the voice they are hearing must be a telepathic communication. It is the only explanation that makes any real sense.

Take now, a clairvoyant working in trance state. They too see a manifestation, but usually their eyes are closed, they then hear the voice of "spirit" yet no-one else hears this sound audibly, so both must be telepathic messages to the clairvoyant.

What about "crisis apparitions"?

A crisis apparition is the report of something happening to a close family member or friend by one person who believes that this person has appeared to them and is in danger or trouble. I can relate a personal story backing up this apparent area of telepathy.

When I was a child I remember waking up in the early hours of the morning hearing my mother screaming – I rushed into her room where my Dad was comforting her. She was saying that she had seen my brother standing at the foot of their bed, in a pair of overalls holding a clip board with papers on it – saying "Mum help". Now my father tried to assure both my mother and me, that it was probably just a bad dream, but Mum was becoming angry as she assured him she knew what she had seen and it was not a dream.

A few minutes later the phone rang, and my father answered it – it was a hospital near Colchester saying that my brother (an HGV 1 driver at the time) had jack-knifed on the A12 in Essex and was in a serious condition at the hospital and that we should attend immediately.

When we finally arrived at the hospital he had regained consciousness and had started to recover, and explained that he was indeed wearing overalls at the time of the accident, which incidentally was EXACTLY the same time that my mother had seen him at the foot of the bed! He also had a clipboard with the documentation for the cargo he was carrying.

Now what other way can anyone explain that vision that my mother had, other than a telepathic link?

Let's also look at an experiment that we tried at West Kennett Long Barrow near Avebury. I stood two sensitives back to back, 20 yards apart, and stood a witness in front of each – one would whisper a number between 1 and 10 to the witness as the "transmitter" the other then would be told to whisper what number he thought the transmitter was thinking of to his witness. The success rate was less than 2 in 10 which is below the average rate for coincidence.

We then placed the same people on a strong energy line that we believe runs through the site and repeated the experiment. This time they scored SEVEN out of ten! Is it possible that the energy frequencies from the Earth actually aided their telepathic abilities? This is certainly an experiment I hope to conduct many more times in the future.

It has long been thought that a strong telepathic link exists between twins, and the work of Guy Lyon-Playfair in London seems to give credence to this theory. In a series of experiments he has conducted and witnessed, he became convinced that there was a strong ability between twins to communicate with each other, often over great distance.

So how can telepathy work, and what can we do to test it within our own lives?

Again, I believe that this is a mind vs brain action, and my belief is that the two entities are indeed very separate. The mind drives our subconscious and allows us to do things without having to really think or concentrate on them. This is I believe, a "right brain initiative" and not many of us make use of the right side of our brains. Whilst I believe that the brain does not CONTROL the mind, we can strengthen our conscious to subconscious link by trying to improve our use of the "right brain".

To give a further idea of the subconscious working in our day-to-day lives, think about when you drive your car for instance. Do you think "I'm going to change gear now", or "I'm going to brake now" – no of course you don't you are more likely to be listening to the radio or talking to a passenger in your car. These actions are done subconsciously.

We also experience our subconscious when we are just waking up or just falling asleep – times at which we are most likely to experience strange phenomena!

Therefore, to test you own telepathic skills try these tests with your partner or family at home:-

Make two sets of six drawings of basic shapes, such as a circle, a square, a triangle, a rectangle, straight line and wavy line. Choose who is to be the "transmitter" and who will be the "receiver" and have a witness in the middle of the room. Position yourselves back to back so that no cheating can take place, and then have the transmitter concentrate on the first of the chosen designs. The transmitter should indicate to the witness which design they are choosing and then should close his/her eyes and try to picture the shape in his/her third eye and imagine sending this vision out into the ether.

The "receiver" should then close his/her eyes and see if they see this picture in their third eye, or see which of the six drawings they feel most drawn towards. When they feel sure they know which one it is, they should show the picture to the witness who will then tell them if it is correct or not. In some circumstances this may work better if they are not told whether they are right or wrong until after the full experiment is finished.

Telekinesis is another form of the use of mental energy, this time being used to move objects using the power of one's own mind, although try as I will, I have never yet been able to achieve success with this!

There are many great publications that deal with telepathy and ESP, and indeed telekinesis in far greater depth and you can also find out a lot more by searching the Internet on these subjects.

If you think you have stronger than average telepathic powers then write to me at ross@phantomorfraud.org.

Twelve
ORBS – The Greatest Debate in Years!

For the past ten or so years, one of the most active debates within paranormal circles, is that of "what is an orb"?

Orbs are circles of light that appear mainly in digital photographs, usually captured during paranormal investigations or in haunted houses.

The sceptics would have us believe that these are either CCD chip faults in digital cameras, dust caught out of focus by the camera's flash, moisture in the air or other airborne particles such as pollen.

The believers meanwhile are convinced that they are the souls of the dead in their basic form prior to a full manifestation.

So who is right?

Well our research shows the latter. It appears that these "orbs" do in many experiments, show an intelligence and move on request of the attendant clairvoyants, and as I have not yet encountered intelligent dust or moisture I have to come down firmly on the side of the believers in this respect.

Whilst filming Ghost Detectives at Derby Gaol, I already told you in an earlier chapter of an experiment that seemed to indicate "orb intelligence" in an experiment we did with clairvoyant Paul Hanrahan. Since then we have repeated that experiment many times with a great deal of success.

Another ongoing and intriguing research area is that of clairvoyants whilst channelling, as they describe the "person" they are seeing, and we often photograph an "orb" in that exact position. Why do we not capture the full entity as the clairvoyant sees them? Could this be because the orb is sending a telepathic picture to the clairvoyant and is actually only there in its basic energy form?

When we die, our human bodies are burned or buried so WHY should we return looking the same way – after all, the soul is probably pure energy and as such would not be recognizable to us and may well take on the form of what we refer to as an orb. If however the orb had telepathic abilities, it could indeed show the receiver an image of how he/she looked in their last human incarnation.

Orbs are not only captured on digital cameras however, I have seen examples on 35mm film, infrared film and even on Polaroid, although these do seem rarer. Why do you think this is? Could it be that the digital photographic spectrum allows for the capture of areas outside of the human eye's capability? Orbs are also caught regularly on video cameras, usually on night vision settings and one of the best examples of this was caught by Mike Cannaby at the Skirrid Inn in Wales.

Photographer Graham Matthews was standing by the side of the bed in what is alleged to be the most haunted room in the building and said something had moved through him and took a photograph. As the flash went off, Mike Cannaby who was filming from the other side of the room, noticed an orb come from the area Graham was standing in and proceeded at great speed towards where Mike was positioned.

Mike could see that this was not a depth of field illusion, as the orb grew larger the closer it got to the video camera before disappearing in front of him.

The pair repeated the experiment a few minutes later and sure enough, as Graham's flash illuminated, another orb shot away from him as if scared by the sudden flash of light. Could these orbs actually be sensitive to light themselves?

We have conducted this experiment on numerous occasions with both camera flashes, and with torches with a good degree of success, and my conclusion is that orbs may well be sensitive to sudden flashes of light. Once again I ask the question of the sceptics, – is dust or moisture sensitive to light?

Going back to our first visit to Bowden House in Devon whilst making the Ghost Detectives programme, the "dancing orb" display was predicted by a clairvoyant sensitive, and if this was just dust explain to me why there was only dust in that room for a couple of hours on one night out of the five we were there?

Also at Bowden, when clairvoyant Paul Hanrahan joined one of the daily ghost tours that were conducted by the then owners of the house Chris and Belinda Petersen, how was it that he indicated that there was a "spirit" walking around on the tour with the group, which he photographed as an orb?

Looking back to another earlier chapter, I told you about the experience of Graham and Andy Matthews on the steps of the Bloody Tower in the Tower of London, with their own "orb experience" – again BOTH of the brothers felt a presence and in that spot an orb was photographed.

If orbs were indeed just dust and moisture, why do they not appear in every picture we take? I have hundreds of holiday snaps, many taken at night with a flash, but no orbs in those.

In another case, I interviewed a nurse who wishes to remain anonymous, but she told me that she had seen "small balls of glowing light" leaving the bodies of people who died in the hospitals where she had worked. She also told me of another nurse who used to open a window every time someone was in the final throws of life, when she asked her why, she said "to let out the soul – the little light that leaves them as they die"!

It would be interesting to set up permanent infrared cameras in operating theatres that could capture what happens whenever someone has a near-death experience, or maybe even cameras over the beds of those who are approaching their last hours of life, so see if science can prove this once and for all. Perhaps one day they will allow us to do this.

In 1907 a doctor from Haverhill, Massachusetts conducted a series of experiments on people who were dying, by placing them on beds set on "scales" and weighing them. He concluded that an average weight loss of 21 grams was lost a few minutes after death which was NOT put down to the excretion of bodily fluids or air exhalation. Dr. Duncan MacDougal believed this to be the departing soul from the human body, stating that this was a energy and as energy is a "mass" it would indeed have weight. Why has this experiment never been repeated?

It seems to me that there is a significant amount of evidence supporting the survival of a soul or energy at the point of bodily death, so why do so many skeptics still insist on denying it as rubbish?

As for the orbs – here's another experiment you can try the next time you are out on a paranormal investigation, or on a ghost tour…..

If you feel a sudden change in temperature or a static electricity "buzz" tell someone with you where you felt it and then take a picture of that exact spot. If you get an orb there it is unlikely to be a coincidence.

I believe that orbs represent one of the biggest breakthroughs in our area of research and one that should not be readily discounted, and although there is still much work to do, the evidence is there for all to see.

Orbs in the back room of Kings Arms.

Closeup of orb at Kings Arms.

Thirteen
EVP – Voices of the Dead?

Now I have to say, that I was on the side of the sceptics on this issue until quite recently.

I was asked to make a DVD documentary about EVP (Electro Voice Phenomena) and interviewed a host of people over the course of the production of the film, as well as taking part in various experiments. The DVD which is still on sale, was called "The Dead ARE Talking" and featured some seemingly incredible recordings of voices of the dead caught on tape and on digital voice recorders.

Now many of the recordings I heard, could have been stray radio waves from taxi ranks or other broadcasts, or even people within the building talking at a distance, but others defied such logical and rational explanation.

Then over Christmas 2005, I had some incredible EVP experiences myself whilst visiting the civil war battlefields in Gettysburg, USA.

Let's start with the documentary.

I took copies of all the EVP's that were given to me by the contributors to the film, and analyzed them on my own PC with a programme you can all freely download on the Internet called "Audacity". This allowed me to take out background noise, check the frequency and wave patterns, and also play the sound to a number of different people to see if they all heard "the same words".

Now this is particularly important when analyzing EVP, as if we are told what is being said, we are prompted to listen for those particular words, whereas if we listen to it without such prompts, we may hear something very different, thus making it more likely to a be a series of chaotic or random data as put forward in the documentary by sceptic Nick Sharratt.

As Nick explains in the documentary, just because someone studies the bible and finds a link between certain words, it doesn't prove a "Bible Code" just that the person has searched very hard, and in the same way a series of random or chaotic sounds on a recording can sound like words to the listener, but often different words to different people listening. What is intriguing is when the voice appears very clear and everyone hears exactly the SAME words.

Also, on numerous recordings, we heard voices close to the microphone and non-room ambient, apparently relating to conversations that others in the room were having at the time, when video has proven that the there was no-one close to the microphone at the time, and no-one in the room saying those words!

In one such case, one of my team leaders for Phantom or Fraud in the north west of England, himself a well respected clairvoyant, captured a number of EVP recordings in an off licence that his team was investigating. In one recording made by Gary Johnson, he was discussing the room the team were in as being a storage area for cigarettes, when a ghostly voice apparently close to the microphone suddenly says "CIGS". This tends to rule out freak radio waves or taxi bleed-over as it was relative to the conversation taking place.

In Gettysburg, I heard numerous EVP's captured by clairvoyant Cathe Curtis, all of which were very clear, and many of which were the sound of gun and cannon fire, so imagine my surprise when she took me out onto the battlefield at dawn one morning during my stay there, and myself and my fiancée Penny both heard cannon fire not only on our EVP recorders but with our own ears! There were no guns firing at the time and the sound was unmistakable.

Whilst conducting a circle (often known as a séance) at a private house in North London a short time ago, one of the ladies at the table said "something just touched my nose". When we later played back the recorder on the table, a female voice replied to that statement with the words "oh sorry". This was not heard by anyone around the table at the time, myself included!

There are many EVP researchers such as Mark Macy in the USA, Judith Chisholm and Mike Rogers here in the UK, all of whom have thousands of recordings of ghostly voices captured on tape and digital machines, some even on answering machines.

Having now studied many of these EVP's at great length, and also now having captured many myself, I am of the opinion that not all of these recordings CAN be explained, and that it could be possible that we're indeed getting communications from beyond the grave, or at the least from a parallel dimension.

Again, this is simple to try at home, just set up a cassette recorder or a digital Dictaphone before you go to bed at night. Ask out loud if there is anyone in the room who would like to leave a message because you would be delighted to hear it. Then leave the machine recording until the tape or memory runs out at which time it will usually turn itself off. Then listen back to it very carefully (preferably with headphones) the next day, and you may just be very surprised at what is on there.

Fourteen
TV's Love of the Sceptics

Have you ever noticed the imbalance on your TV screens when it comes to paranormal TV shows?

The greatest majority of TV shows about the paranormal, contain a sceptical bias and feature the "rent-a-sceptic" brigade of Professor Chris French, Dr. Richard Wiseman and James Randi.

The TV watchdogs have various codes about paranormal style programming and the general overview of this is that pro-paranormal features should be balanced with a sceptical viewpoint to keep a balance, however anti-paranormal programmes do not require such a balance with the believers viewpoint. Now forgive me if I'm wrong here, but I find that wholly unfair.

When we made the Ghost Detectives series, they sat Professor French in front of monitors in a studio and had him put forward theories for rational and logical explanation of all the paranormal activity that took place during the filming of the six shows. Now as he wasn't present at ANY of the filming, how on earth can he make statements like "well this was probably dust" or "this could have been a stray light source from a window" or words to that effect?

If indeed the "dancing orbs" were just explainable as dust, don't you think WE would have put that argument forward as indeed we DID in the Pengersick Castle programme, where it was obvious what we were seeing was not genuine orb activity.

Also, I would add that if there was dust in that room at Bowden House, how come it only appeared ONCE in five days and nights of filming?

I watch shows like those made by Derren Brown which tend to rubbish clairvoyance and general paranormal research, but I would say this to Mr. Brown – Just because you can replicate something – it does not mean that the original does not exist.

In the Channel 4 programme "Psychic Secrets Revealed" made by Objective Productions, they managed to use some of the footage from Ghost Detectives from the owners of the rights and completely dismissed our orb footage, yet gave us NO OPPORTUNITY to balance the opinion of their sceptics with our own defence! They also failed to broadcast any moving orbs on video in this production, I wonder why that was?

I once approached a commissioning editor on a terrestrial TV channel and pitched an idea for a new paranormal TV series and she looked at me as if I was an alien from the planet Zwog and said patronizingly "this is SO not me, ghosts do not exist and I would not subject my viewers to such rubbish"! Suddenly even TV commissioners are experts on the paranormal. I note that this woman no longer works for the channel. Who makes the choices for you the TV viewer? It seems that SHE knows better than you as to what you'd like to see on your screens.

When we did the live show from Charlton House for ITV2, we had to pre-record any "séances" which then had to be approved for broadcast before the transmission. One has to ask WHY? Are we still in the dark ages?

"Orbcatcher" Andy Matthews felt a presence at Charlton House, and took this photo witnessed by Producer Simon Moorhead

Orb appearing at Charlton House

Dr. Richard Wiseman, a former magician and conjurer, enjoys showing people how they can be "conned" by fake clairvoyants using basic magic tricks, and whilst I would agree that there are many clairvoyant mediums who are NOT the "real thing" this is a terrible blow for the real mediums who really do appear to have a gift. How many times though, has Wiseman been given TV airtime to discuss and promote this view.

There is a lot of money to be earned in television by being a sceptic, so one has to ask the question that if confronted by 100% proof of the existence of the paranormal, would they EVER admit to having their views changed?

As for TV, some praise must go to digital station Living TV for their success with programmes such as Most Haunted, for the promotion it has given to the paranormal, and the fact that it has brought the matter to the larger public's attention, but we should never lose sight of the fact that this is an entertainment programme on an entertainment channel, and should not in any way be taken as serious paranormal research.

I really think that now we are in the 21st century, television should recognise that this is an area of science and more programmes should be made showing the real research and evidence that is being produced by groups including doctors and scientists from all over the world, without the ridicule of the rent-a-sceptic brigade. Let the audience make their own minds up on the evidence that is there for all to see.

It would also be nice to see some of that valuable TV money finding its way into the pro-paranormal research coffers rather than the hands of the sceptics, as it seems most of the grant monies already head their way.

Fifteen
My Clash with James Randi & His Followers

If you haven't heard of James Randi, he is an author and sceptic based in the USA and has, through his organization, put up a reward of US $1 Million for anyone who can PROVE the existence of the paranormal.

A couple of years ago, I added a section to my web site at www.phantomorfraud.org about dowsing, and how I was convinced that it worked, when I received a direct challenge from a member of Randi's discussion forums challenging me to go for Randi's Million Dollar reward!

Having read the terms of the challenge, I felt that nobody would ever get past stage 1, because of the way the rules were written and felt that the challenge was set up in such a way that the money would never be paid out. To date I have been proven right, as no-one has yet managed to get to the second stage of the challenge, as far as I am aware.

Instead, I challenged Mr. Randi to come to the UK and spend six weeks in ACTUAL haunted venues with my team, and said that I believed I could change his views. I said that if I did, he should donate £100,000 to our research and the balance of the fund to charities of my choice.

Mr. Randi e-mailed me and said "you're probably right" but refused to take up my challenge despite me offering to cover all his travel and accommodation costs at the time.

Now one must ask WHY Mr. Randi was so keen NOT to have the evidence put in front of him on OUR terms?

I then became the target of many verbal attacks in Randi's forum by his supporters egged on by the person who had initially contacted me about dowsing.

I have since spoken to various parties who have taken part in, applied for or considered Randi's challenge, and so far have not had one of them saying the challenge was fair and achievable.

Now I would ask, why hasn't someone put up a million dollars to fund the research of people such as Professor Gary Schwartz, or Dr. Sam Parnia? Their work is already showing evidence of soul survival – yet they struggle to get any funding for further studies.

I am sure Mr. Randi is genuine in his beliefs and I feel sure that his challenge will continue to create interest in the paranormal, and for that he should be praised, but I personally do not see that US$1 million ever being paid out!

I have watched Mr. Randi in various TV documentaries and believe that like Professor French, Dr. Wiseman and Susan Blackmore, he would need an absolute miracle to happen in front of his eyes to change his opinions, but maybe one day it will.

Randi is by no means the only hardened sceptic out there – and they have as much right to their beliefs as we do as believers, but if I could change just one thing, it would be to have them open their eyes and their minds to the fact that there ARE things out there that defy current rational or logical explanation.

I have done various radio interviews where I have been pitted against the likes of Professor Chris French and Tony Youens etc, and I always feel that their sceptical arguments are so much weaker than ours as believers, but maybe I'm just biased.

I do hope however, that my radio show Now THAT'S Weird (www.nowthatsweird.co.uk) will help redress the balance, by being a "pro-paranormal" talk show where believers can air their own views, experiences and research without ridicule from the sceptic army. Everyone I believe, has a right to free speech on matters such as this, and I like to let my listeners decide what they think of the arguments being put forward.

For too long now, believers have had to put up with ridicule and teasing by media reporters and presenters, purely because what they believe does not fit in with the accepted "norm".

I remember being a guest on one local radio show in England, with Prof Chris French where he was introduced as a University professor of great knowledge and I was introduced as a "nutter who believes in ghosts". That said, by the end of the interview I think I had even made the presenter eat his words and think again.

I am happy to open dialogue with any sceptic who is willing to keep an open mind, and one good thing I will say about Chris French is that he has been willing to join us on an investigation with an open mind, unlike Mr Randi.

Sixteen
Re-incarnation - Surely Not Another 70 Years?

Re-incarnation – well I for one wouldn't want to have to suffer another 70 years on this plane. But could it be an explanation for past life memories and de-ja-vu?

I have always side-stepped this issue in the past, as its not an area that I really had any views on until about a year ago when I met an interesting guy in my local pub.

For the sake of his anonymity, we shall call him John…

I first met John when I moved into a 16th century thatched cottage in a small Devon village close to Okehampton. John lived just opposite and was a regular in the village pub a few doors down from me.

John was a very well educated man, and quite quiet. It took some time to get him to open up to me, but eventually we struck up a friendship, and I became aware of his own study and interest in the scientific side of paranormal research. His interest in past-life regression and reincarnation however, came about almost by accident.

John told me that he had sought the services of a hypnotherapist in bid for pain control for a debilitating illness. Little did he realize that his appointment was to provide him with an experience he will never forget.

This is John's memory of events as he related them to me.

Under hypnosis, I suddenly said; "Mr. Hodgkin, that man may be the sodomizing son of a poxed Plymouth whore, but by God he can handle this ship"...... at which point the hypnotherapist went for the tape recorder!

I was asked to describe what I could see. I gave the year as 1796, and I was at sea off Portsmouth, trailing a vessel which I described as a 28-gun Frigate, name Ariadne. I gave my name as Johnson or Johnston.

On being brought forward a few years, I found myself dining in a large Georgian room. I described the meal. I realized that I was in fact in a house about which I have had very vivid dreams since a very early age. When old enough not to be frightened by the dreams, I had begun to explore the house, but was never able to get through a doorway at the end of a corridor. Even under hypnosis, I realized that the dining room in which I was sitting was the room at the other side of the door....

On the tape, I grumble about the cook; " First remove is salmon - at least the grass-combing lubber can't bugger that up - or can he? Venison to follow..." If I were to be taken to the house now (it's somewhere in Hampshire, I should imagine), I would know my way around it.....

Afterwards, I decided the tape was just ramblings, but thought I would check anyway. I could find no reference to any HMS Ariadne until much later (1840s), and was on the point of dismissing the whole thing as nonsense when I suddenly discovered an entry for 'Ariadne, 32 guns, launched Portsmouth 1795, Captain Johnson'.....

The discrepancy in guns is explained because some people only referred to the broadside guns, of which there would have been 28, and ignored the 'chasers' in the bow and stern, of which there would have been four. Thus HMS Victory is variously described as a 100-gun ship or a 104-gun ship.....

HMS Ariadne disappears from the records after Trafalgar in 1805. There is no record of her having been wrecked, taken or sunk, so it would seem likely that she would have been sold out of the service as she was quite small for a frigate, most of which by then carried broadsides of 36 guns or more.

Now this story intrigued me, as I by now knew John well enough to know that he is nobody's fool, and would have immediately looked for all the rational and logical explanations to explain his experience. He was however convinced beyond doubt when he spoke to me, that he had lived before and that this experience was proof of the fact.

There are many such stories from other people that have been regressed, together with those who have living memory of past life events that they could not of known about at the time.

I also believe that time as we know it, may not be linear, but in fact CIRCULAR, which would mean that at certain points on the circle, we may align closer with the parallel dimension to a past life existence, and thus the memories grow stronger.

If we imagine for a moment, a dimension full of souls of those who have passed from this existence, it would be a very crowded place wouldn't it? However, if as each new birth takes place, a soul enters the new born child, then the same souls would be forming a circular time motion throughout past, present and future.

John's experience was one that made me realize that nothing should ever be discounted or denied without first looking at all the evidence available.

Seventeen
So You're Dead, Why Come Back Here?

Now I suppose one should ask the question that if you die, why would you want to return back here as a "ghost"? Perhaps this is why so many "pubs" are allegedly haunted – after all its as good a place as any to return to I suppose.

Many spiritualists and clairvoyants believe that a sudden death such as a murder, suicide or car accident etc., can leave the spirit either not believing they have died, or refusing to "move into the light" and therefore remaining on this plane.

Others believe that such a large outbreak of emotion can be captured within the walls of a building and under certain conditions, can play back like a 3D video recording.

There appear to be three main different types of "haunting" such as "residual haunting" where the building holds a memory, an "interactive haunting" where the spirit communicates with us and seems to be very aware of our presence, and a "past-time replay" where the ghost seems to be unaware of other presences and performs the same movement every time it is seen.

When we were filming part of the Ghost Detectives series at Marsden Grotto, one "spirit" was asked during a channeling session with clairvoyant Paul Hanrahan, "why do you stay here" and he replied "why do YOU stay in your home?". Maybe that in itself is the explanation we seek – that they just return to the place they loved the most? The spirit in question was alleged to be that of Jack "The Blaster" Bates, the man who built Marsden Grotto.

If however, we think again about the possible existence of parallel dimensions, then maybe the spiritual plane is right alongside our own, and many spirits can cross over quiet easily?

But what about PEOPLE who are haunted rather than places?

Maybe, most of these can be explained by split personalities and psychiatric disorders, but some cases of possession and poltergeist activity, seem to defy that simple explanation.

Where possession is of a "demonic nature" I firmly believe that most cases do have a psychiatric explanation, and I think there is little firm evidence to suggest that demons really exist. After all, it was Christianity that invented demons and devils, and most "possessions" are brought into the public arena not by researchers like myself but by the church. One must ask whether this provides good PR for religious belief?

Where a person is commonly seeing a dead relative or friend around them, this I find far more intriguing, especially in cases where clairvoyants appear to communicate knowledge that the living survivor could not have known. For instance, where something was hidden by the deceased and the clairvoyant passes on a message whereby the survivor finds the item.

Quite often, these "hauntings" appear to be for one of two reasons:-

1) They have unfinished business, such as a message or item as above to be discovered after which they then pass into the light and move on.

2) The are sent back as a spirit guide or guardian to watch over the person.

Whether you believe or disbelieve either of these explanations, there does seem to be a growing number of cases of people being haunted rather than the house or home.

Let's look for a moment at the matter of "spirit guides". I once sat down with a lady and started to describe the person I felt was with her, whom I described as a guide. I gave a very strong description of what she looked like in life, what she did for a living, what the relationship was with this person, and how and when she died.

Now I had never met this woman before, and could not have known any of this information, but it was all 100% correct and was a description of her best friend who had passed away after a long battle against cancer, only a few months prior to our chat. Could it be that her best friend remained with her as a guardian and guide?

Many people believe that their spirit guides are relations or friends who return to keep an eye on them, but if this is indeed true – then did they not have a guide BEFORE that person passed, or do we get changes in our spirit guides form time to time?

Figure forming

Clairvoyants believe that their spirit guides were often very spiritual people in life such as native Americans or shaman, but I personally prefer to think that our guides are connected with our own history, family line or possible past-lives. After all, we hear a lot of talk about "soul mates" and perhaps if re-incarnation is real, then we are surrounded by the same people in each existence?

So where would you return to when you die, if you could choose? Perhaps you'd haunt someone who has made your life hell? Perhaps you'd stay alongside a loved one? How about the pub?

I think for me, I'd like to think I may move onto something better than this life, although the thought of creating a poltergeist style havoc around an ex wife could be quite appealing!

There have been many examples of deceased loved ones inexplicably appearing in photographs with family and friends, how do we explain this? On many occasions it is just a photographic anomaly, but I have seen many cases where the image is far too clear and does not appear to the experts to have been tampered with or manipulated in any way, so is this another way that spirit can make contact, and if so why?

Again I refer to a theory I put forward earlier in this book, that when we leave the human form, we do not and CAN NOT look like we did in life, so how can we manifest in our former bodily shape if not by telepathy? In which case, how would we project an image onto a camera or into a photographic scene?

I think it was Arthur C. Clarke who once said "the universe is not only stranger than we imagine, but stranger than we CAN imagine". Is it the case therefore, that our human brain is designed only for this existence, and unable therefore to cope with the real explanations of what lay beyond?

If we do return to this plane in our spiritual form, is it in fact in a new born baby to begin another reincarnation?

We are still a long way from an explanation to any of these questions, but the research continues.

Eighteen
Parallel Dimensions - An Answer or a Confusion?

The theory that we live in a series of parallel dimensions is by no means a new one, but it does offer some very differing explanations for various areas of strange phenomena investigation.

Let's just assume for a moment, that "ghosts" are in fact the "living" in a parallel dimension, and that through a series of natural events, break through the wafer thin gauze that may separate these dimensions. Could they appear through a kind of interference as a ghostly vision to us?

If that were the case, could we appear in the same way, totally unknowingly to us, in their dimension?

In the bible, Jesus was quoted as saying "in my father's house there are many mansions" – could he have been talking about multiple dimensions?

In the book of Enoch, the Patriarch relates to visiting multiple dimensions. Could one of these multiple dimensions be the very place we move to when we die? Could this be the "spirit realm" that we hear so much about, and if so, is "Heaven" actually here on earth?

Well I'm not a religious person, although I do believe in a God or creator figure, but feel that the worse thing that ever happened to Christianity was Christians themselves. What were believed to be the original holy texts, have long since been re-written by more earthly individuals, and many of the world's wars have been fought over religion, so I see little reason to attend a building that on many occasions is full of hypocrites, to talk to the creator.

My own experiences of the church has been of people who are so obviously not without their own sins, preaching to me about mine!

But back to parallel dimensions……

Many people have reported seeing what they believe to be ghosts, and many have also reported seeing what they believe to be "time-slips" – whole scenery changes around them apparently dating back to past times. Now what if they were actually seeing a parallel dimension?

One area my research studied for over two years, was the time period that clairvoyants were "channeling". It appeared that most "spirits" that they were bringing through, were from the period 1700 – 1850. We didn't seem to be getting any cavemen, Egyptian rulers or medieval knights, so why JUST this time period.

One theory is that time is circular and we rotate around our own past and future like a clock face, thus if this be the case, we could maybe be born into our own future or past in reincarnation.

Another perhaps more plausible theory, is that the nearest parallel dimension to our own, is that of a time period 1700 – 1850. This also appears to be the period that most "time slips" seem to show.

If someone actually LIVING in that time period but in a separate dimension, is brought forward by a clairvoyant who just happens to be working on that frequency, maybe this is why they "do not know they are dead" – because they are NOT!

In an investigation we conducted at Chicksands Priory in Bedfordshire, we saw a chandelier swaying to one side, and then stopping before moving to the other side. We called in one of the clairvoyants on the team who said that there was a maid there cleaning it. Could this "maid" have been a living person form a parallel dimension?

At the Lilley Arms in Hertfordshire, the landlady confronted a ghostly man sitting at one of the tables after the bar had closed and asked "why are you here in my home" – the entity replied "I think it you madam that is in MY home"! Could this again be a slip between the dimensions?

Let's look at the Loch Ness legend for a moment.

Many believe that the Loch Ness monster is no more than a rumor spread by the locals to encourage tourists, but photographs do seem to show something unusual in the water, almost ghostly in it's appearance. Now what if "Nessie" was in fact swimming around happily in his/her own dimension, but on rare occasions slipped through into our dimension, could this explain the strange phenomena?

Loch Ness has a very powerful Earth energy line that runs across it from Urquart Castle across to Boleskine on the other side of the Loch. Boleskine was apparently chosen by Alastair Crowley for a magic ritual because of its "awesome power" – could Crowley have known of the strange phenomena that occurred there, and more to the point did he believe it to be a gateway between the dimensions?

The graveyard at Boleskine cemetery appears to have a number of what may be Knights Templar gravestones – and they too believed that they should be buried near to "gateways" to the other side. Did they have knowledge of these doorways between dimensions?

What about alien entities?

Man people have photographs that seem to have an alien image in them, I myself have one. Whilst conducting an investigation at Rendelsham Forest some years ago, I described something I felt hovering over me as an entity "not of this world". One of my team took a picture and above my head was an alien looking creature. He could not have tampered with the picture, as he ran it off the camera to his laptop in front of me in his car on site! (I cannot publish this picture as he would not allow it to be published I'm afraid.)

Now could it be the case, that these "aliens" are also part of a parallel dimension, and NOT traveling light years across space to visit us? But if that were the case, why the need for flying machines, unless of course they too were crossing the dimensional barrier to occasionally be seen in our skies.

So perhaps the search for extraterrestrial life forms should be concentrated a little closer to home?

There has also been much talk of "stargates" and other doorways used by our ancestors to move between different points across distance. But could these also have been inter-dimensional transfer points? It sounds far-fetched, and more like something out of a science fiction novel, but then who would have thought mobile phones could have been a reality fifty years ago?

The research into parallel dimensions intrigues me, and I think offers our best chance of finding answers in the years to come.

Ninteen
Dowsing or When is a Ley Line NOT a Ley Line?

For many years, I had been told that ley lines were energy forms that represented various parts of the color spectrum, such as yellow for spirit energy, green for earth energy, black for bad energy etc. My own research tends to debunk ALL of that.

I can put down a "ley line" and pick it back up again, and regularly show this experiment on my raining courses for all to see. In fact when I was filming at Bowden House in Devon, I did the experience with John Bowers a member of Devon Dowsers, who was astonished to find a ley line with his dowsing rods, that I had put down in front of the TV camera crew only minutes before.

Dowser, John Bowers at Bowden House

My belief is that ley lines were put down by our elders, when there were no roads, as a way of route-mapping, so that they could find their way back across forests and unknown terrain.

Energy lines however, are very different. I cannot put down or pick up an energy line, which appears to be linked to geographic fault lines across the world. These energy lines are often found in areas where there is a lot of paranormal activity, crop circles and UFO sightings, so could there be a link?

So how do we tell the difference….

Well dowsing works, I have no doubt of that, although how it works is still somewhat of a puzzle. I personally believe that these energy lines, and indeed ley lines, transmit a frequency of some kind that we can tune into and pick up when dowsing. The subconscious then sends a small electronic impulse to the hand which thus creates a movement in the dowser's rods or crystal.

Many dowsers will argue different reasons as to how it works, but they all agree that it DOES work. Many are employed to find sources of water and underground water mains, some are employed by archeologists to find ancient sites and ruins long buried into the ground, and I even heard tale of a woman in South Africa who is paid fortunes by diamond mining companies for dowsing for new sites. Apparently her success rate is amazing!

The skeptics will argue that ley lines do not exist at all, and that dowsing is a work of luck or coincidence, but I feel there is far too much evidence out there to dismiss this quite so easily.

So how can we PROVE the existence of energy lines? This is a lot harder, as there is not yet any form of test equipment that seems able to detect these very different forms of energy.

There have been a lot of different references in the past to ley lines in books like Alfred Watkins' The Old Straight Track, and even in the more recent "Dragon Project" where they were referred to as "Dragon lines". But few people have until now identified the difference between the ley lines and the seemingly natural Earth energy lines.

I recently did a talk to Devon Dowsers and was amazed not to be heckled or told that they disagreed with my theories. It seems that word had gone round about my experiment with John Bowers, and another dowser there even was as bold as to say "Ross – when I met you and you asked me to rethink the way I dowsed, you changed the whole way I operated – thank you".

So let's talk about dowsing. Dowsing is an ancient art, used for many different reasons, although greatly popular for finding underground sources of water.

Usually, the dowser will use either brass or copper L shaped dowsing rods, a Y shaped branch or stick, or a crystal pendulum on a chain.

For me, I started with a pair of wire coat-hangers bent into L shapes and with two BIC biro holders as handles to avoid me being easily able to turn the rods.

You should clear your mind and walk forward slowly with the rods held out in front of you ideally about 12 inches apart. The best place to start is in your own garden looking for an underground water pipe or sewer. Ask the question either in your mind or audibly "show me the water pipe". Walk across the area where you know the water supply to be and see if the rods turn on their own at one spot. If they do, walk from the other side of the garden and see if they find the same spot. You will probably be very surprised to see that they do, and that this is in fact EXACTLY where the water pipe runs.

There are many local dowsing clubs you can find on the Internet where you can then try this out further with other like-minded individuals.

But dowsing is not only confined to a search for water. Good dowsers can find missing jewelry, energy lines, ley lines, underground electric cables and even buried artifacts!

I was doing a live radio show in Buckinghamshire a short while back, and in the room next door, Haunting Breaks who were sponsoring the show, were training people who had come along for a different kind of weekend away, in how to prepare for a night of paranormal investigation. I could hear raucous laughter coming from the room, and sent one of my helpers over to find out what was going on.

They were learning how to dowse! The laughter was coming from a room full of skeptics and open-minded people who were absolutely amazed that the rods were actually moving for them.

There is no trick to it, and it's not just something done by trained professionals, anyone can dowse – try it at home and see for yourself.

So how can you use dowsing at a paranormal investigation you may ask…..

In the same way as I described above, you can locate the energy source that may be linked to activity in the building you are investigating. Simply walk across a room, first asking "show me the energy line" and then the same again this time asking "show me spirit energy".

I was extremely surprised the first time I found "spirit energy". A clairvoyant had told me that there was a female spirit in the room, but didn't tell me where and asked me to dowse for her. The clairvoyant had told a third party as a witness where the woman was standing before I had entered the room.

I dowsed the room asking the question "show me the female spirit in this room" to my utter disbelief the rods crossed in the exact spot where the woman had been seen by the clairvoyant and confirmed by the witness.

Still unsure whether this was coincidence, I went and found another team member in a different part of the building who had no idea of the experiment that had just taken place, and asked him to dowse for a "spirit energy" in the same room. The clairvoyant confirmed that the spirit was still standing in the same spot, and low and behold the investigator's rods crossed in exactly the same place.

This is something I now do regularly at investigations, and it not only confirms what the mediums tell me, but also tells us the best places to position our cameras for the investigation ahead.

Dowsing, I believe, plays a major part in the investigation of strange phenomena.

You can buy dowsing rods and crystals in most new age shops, although my advice is that it works just as well with two bent coat hangers, so why spend the money?

As for crystal dowsing, I believe that a metal pendulum on a piece of string works just as well as any crystal, but it is better if it is shaped to a point at the end.

There is a lot of conflicting information on dowsing on the Internet, but there are also some very good sites that will help you develop your dowsing skills.

http://www.dowsing.com (Bill Cox)
http://www.britishdowsers.org
http://www.diviningmind.com
http://dowsingtips.com/dowsing.html
http://www.hamishmiller.co.uk/dowsing.asp   (Hamish Miller)

Twenty
Investigations & Stories
Moments that Changed My Thinking

There are many paranormal investigations that I have attended or organized, that have changed my very thinking on the paranormal. In this chapter, I will outline some of the experiences that have stood out for me and made me realize that not everything HAS a rational explanation.

I was on an investigation at the old derelict Barnes Hospital in Cheadle near Manchester, with a group of our best investigators over two days and nights. The place was boarded up but had been broken into on regular occasions by drug users, and for this reason, I had made a firm rule that NO investigator was to work alone, and groups of three were formed. This was not only to safeguard against possible problems with the LIVING, but also so that any paranormal activity could be witnessed by more than just one person.

The only time, it was acceptable for investigators to move around the building alone was to access the car park via an exit very close to the main control area, which was covered by part of the CCTV system we had rigged up.

On the second night of the investigation, I was going to get something from my car, when I noticed a door open at the end of a corridor in front of me, and what looked like Nita Grant one of my investigators walk through alone and into a side room. I immediately ran down the corridor to ask why she had separated from her group. As I approached said door, it opened and through came Nita with her two fellow group members. So who did I see walk through the door before her?

Assuming it may be an intruder I entered the side room off the corridor to confront the person, but there was no-one in the room. The windows were bordered up and there were no other exits from the room. Nita and her group had followed me in and noticed that I looked somewhat shocked, and I explained to them what I had just seen.

We all examined the room carefully, looking for secret or hidden exits, and trying to see if there was any way a person could have left this room without being seen. The answer was NO.

Nita then asked me if I had switched the light on in the room, I said no. She then pointed out that the light was OFF when they left the control room to conduct their experiments in this area of the building.

Unfortunately, this was one area of the hospital that was not covered by our CCTV cameras, as being limited to the number we had available, we had chosen to put them up in the areas where the clairvoyants amongst the team had felt there was the highest chance of paranormal activity.

Normally after an occurrence like this, we awake the next morning with a whole series of possible explanations as to what it may have been that we witnessed – but I could think of nothing that would rationally explain the figure I so clearly saw walking into that room.

I honestly believe, on that night, I witnessed my first full body apparition.

Now I mentioned in an earlier chapter about Bowden House in Totnes, Devon, where we filmed the first show in the Ghost Detectives series. This is probably my favorite "haunted" location.

I was still very skeptical when I first visited Bowden, but the voice of the child whispering in my ear, certainly spooked me! But there was a lot of other activity there that made me think again about whether the paranormal did indeed exist.

One such example was the candle incident. If you watched the programme and saw the candle flame lift off the candle, rise about six inches into the air, go out, then re-light and slowly return back down to rejoin the wick – you probably thought it was a special effect. It wasn't – we all watched in amazement from the control room as this happened.

It almost seemed to happen in slow-motion, in a room that was locked-off so that no one would enter or leave and disturb the energies that had been reported in the Great Hall.

This candle was on the very same table where the "dancing orb display" was to take place later the same day!

I have never witnessed anything like this, and cannot offer any explanation as to how a flame from a candle can rise off the wick, continue to burn, go out and then re-light in mid-air before slowly returning to the wick.

On another investigation near Bolton, I witnessed yet more convincing "paranormal activity".

Area team leader Gary Johnson had pulled-off a real coup, in getting us the keys to a whole deserted village. It was owned entirely by the children's charity NCH – who had shut down a school in the village where all the local houses were provided for staff and school buildings. We had access to everywhere.

Once again my experience centered around investigator Nita Grant.

Using her own clairvoyance skills she had explained the presence of three ghostly children in an upstairs room of one of the buildings. This was also confirmed by fellow investigator Amanda Sheppard who had picked up on the same information.

Sceptic Philip Kimpton was filming in the room as Nita began to converse with the "children". Suddenly, investigators in the room began reporting orbs around Nita, myself included.

After some time talking to the "children" and getting to know their names, Nita asked if they would help her with a little experiment, to which they apparently agreed. Nita then asked one child to move to her left and sit with Penny and another to move to the right towards me on the other side of the room.

Philip suddenly exclaimed "bloody hell I don't believe what I am seeing" – he could see the orbs moving on his video in the exact directions that Nita had stated. I hurriedly took a photo of Penny sitting opposite me, and low and behold, there appeared to be a glowing ball of light sitting on her lap!

Now my first thought was that this could be a "depth of field" anomaly where it appeared to be on her lap but could have actually been something much closer to the lens of the camera, but when another investigator in a totally different position in the room confirmed the orb on Penny's lap in HIS picture, we all knew that this had to be more than a photographic anomaly. Indeed if it was DUST then we have to say dust has intelligence!

Nita was not all surprised at what had happened, she senses the children moving around the room.

The night before this had happened, I had taken a picture of the front of this particular building and there was a bright orb on the inside of the window, part of it obscured by the window frame, as if perhaps a child was watching me from the window of that very same room.

Another memorable night was that of our investigation at the Wellington Hotel in Boscastle in Cornwall.

I had sat with the clairvoyant team in a "séance circle" and whilst not much had occurred, I could not have imagined what was to happen right after we stood up.

I was talking to sceptic David Connolly who was one of our investigation team who had traveled over from Ireland and I suddenly stopped, raised me camera and said to David "I have just been told to take two pictures down the bar here, the voice said "Now you see me – now you don't".

I proceeded to take two photos in quick succession on my Nikon 950 Coolpix digital camera. In the first there was a very bright, large, glowing, BLUE orb. In the second in exactly the same place, there was nothing.

I showed the pictures to David who was somewhat surprised, and admitted he had no explanation. David admitted at the end of the investigation that his mind had been opened to many things he had experienced that he could not explain. Another sceptic bites the dust.

On a trip to Scotland, I was taken to a ruin of an old monastery or church, by a local man who wanted to meet me to discuss the Knights Templars in Caithness. He took me into what remained of this building and I immediately started to pick up on someone who said his name was "Sir John".

I told him where he was standing and took a photo. An orb appeared in the very spot I had pointed out only seconds before. He turned to Penny who was with me, shook his head and then looked back at me and said whilst examining the photo "why did you have to go and do that? There was I convinced that orbs were all dust and now you have to go and do that"!

He later told me that the building had been commissioned by a "Sir John" who was heavily associated with the area. I can't remember the surname, but it certainly left him far more open-minded than he had been when I first arrived.

Whilst on a guided tour of Mary Kings Close in Edinburgh, I had felt the presence of a spirit following me throughout the tour. The guide had said that we were not allowed to take photographs, which I found very irritating as I wanted more proof.

As we walked from room to room I became more and more aware of a young woman's presence and desperately wanted to take a photo to see if yet again, the orb appeared in the right place.

I drifted to the back of the group and started to lag a little behind, and as the group turned a corner I told Penny there was someone behind me, and I took a photo – low and behold – the orb was in the centre of the photograph. I thanked the spirit and moved on to rejoin the group with a wry smile on my face, as Penny looked in astonishment at the photograph.

In a more recent case in Monkokehampton, a small village in West Devon, I was asked by a regular at my local pub, to investigate a presence he was feeling in the 600 year old house he was renting.

On entering the building, I felt not one, but TWO presences, and began to tell him what I was getting. The man was not associated with the house, but farming nearby and may have been bringing meat or supplies to the house. He may also have been working in the grounds.

The other presence however, I was certain was connected with the house next door, and I begin to give her name, a description and relayed that this was once one big house, and that the wall she walked through into his bedroom, used to be a doorway. I also said that she stood watching him from the end of his bed.

He nodded as he had admitted that he DID sense her watching him as he lay in his bed at night, but he couldn't say at the time if the name or description were right.

A couple of days later I received a text on my mobile phone which read "correct on all counts, house used to be one big place, name of woman and description was bang-on and it was the mother of the old lady next door!!" He apparently had been around to his neighbor to ask if he knew who had lived there in the past, and eventually admitted that he wanted to find out about a "ghost".

On an investigation at the Red Lion pub in Exbourne in Devon, we encountered a number of very strange things happening.

During a séance at around 2 a.m. one of the clairvoyants asked for a "sign" that spirit were present, and at that exact moment the phone behind the bar began ringing but not in the normal way, just one long continuous ring like a fire alarm. The landlord picked up the phone but there was no-one there, he put it back on the receiver and it continue to ring for several minutes before finally stopping. It had never done it before, and has never done it again since.

Just after the séance, a heavy bar access point crashed down with an almighty thud. Again this had never happened before, nor again since.

The night's activities were witnessed by a reporter from Devon Life Magazine, who admitted to being somewhat "freaked" by the things that had happened.

I had also again taken a number of pictures of "orbs" In the exact spots where the clairvoyants were sensing presences.

A regular at the pub who has an interest in the paranormal, joined us for the investigation, and twice said he saw a woman in a Victorian style dress walking in the top of the bar area near the pool table, the very area where I had also just picked up on a "female presence".

Berry Pomeroy Castle in Devon is a well known haunting, so I was very enthusiastic to visit the place on a day out with Penny soon after moving to Devon.

Having spent the afternoon roaming around the ruins of the castle I was a little deflated that I hadn't picked up on anything, when all of a sudden I felt myself drawn to the gardens. Here I encountered "the blue lady".

I told Penny that the lady was showing herself to me in blue, usually a visual representation of sadness, and that she was holding a baby but at arms length as if she wanted me to take it form her. She was looking at the child in disgust as if it was something nasty of evil.

Penny went to the shop and bought a guide book to see if there was anything about the ghosts of the castle, and her face almost went white as she started to read about a "lady in blue" who was regularly seen in the gardens holding a baby. It appears that the baby was the result of her being raped and abused by her own Father – hence the probable look of disgust on her face at the child.

A little while after this, Penny took me to Powderham Castle in Devon, and we joined a "tour" of the building. As we were about to enter a large room, I said I had a girl standing next to me, and gave Penny a name, saying that it was one of the three sisters. As we entered the room the tour guide showed us a massive painting of three sisters on the wall, and one of them was the name I had given to Penny just moments before. I cannot remember the name off the top of my head, but it was an unusual name and not one that a person guessing names would have come up with!

Penny smiled as the tour guide gave the information. I guess she was getting to know that her boyfriend was a bit different than most other people.

Going back to investigations, I still have very fond memories of the apparent ghost of Jack "the blaster" Bates at Marsden Grotto. I knew from the moment I arrived that his spirit was with me and he provided me I am sure with a great number of very good orb photos at the venue, which was apparently his former home.

I mentioned Jack earlier in this book, and his appearance at Margate Theatre Royal telling us that he wanted to speak to me the following week at "his home". I honestly believe he DID talk to me, and I also believe he showed himself on the video camera....

Whilst looking through some video footage for something else, we noticed an apparition apparently walking through a wall on a staircase. This "apparition" could only be seen in fast forward search or fast reverse search and not in normal play or pause, and as such defied the laws of time as we know it. This we describe as "temporal time" and I believe that Jack Bates was helping me to provide yet further evidence of paranormal existence.

In Gettysburg over the Christmas holiday in 2005, I encountered more evidence of strange activity at the home of medium Cathe Curtis and photographer Rick Fulton.

We were staying with the couple for Christmas, and had already been warned of a "warm welcome from their nonpaying guests" (that's what Cathe calls her spirits). From the moment we arrived the wall clock in their living room started going BACKWARDS!

One night Penny woke me up in the middle of the night and said "Ross cuddle me" I said what's up and she replied "don't ask, just do it". Well I knew by the tone of her voice that she had been spooked, so I continued to question her and she finally admitted "things are moving about over there".

I wasn't particularly surprised as I had witnessed this myself the night before, and had also seen lights suddenly coming on inside the wardrobes in the room.

Also whilst we were there, we were called into the room where we were staying one evening to witness an incredible cold mist developing. It was so cold we could see our own breath. Some visiting friends of Cathe's were also there and witnessed the phenomena, which a few moments later had dissipated.

On one of my live radio shows from Gettysburg at an old orphanage, we suddenly heard footsteps in the room above us, and sent two people up to see who had walked into the premises which had been locked after we entered. There was no-one there, yet the mysterious ghostly footsteps continued.

The Swan in Markyate near Dunstable in Bedfordshire was another place that had some surprises in store for us. The landlady's daughter had run out of the pub screaming just a few nights before telling her mother that there was a ghost in her room!

Apparently, like most teenage girls, she had come to stay with her Mum and had emptied her clothes across the floor of the room. When she returned to the room after a drink with her Mum in the bar, all the clothes were neatly folded and stacked on the end of the bed.

Thinking that her Mother had done it, in protest she knocked them all back to the floor. She rushed downstairs to shout at her Mum, suddenly realizing that she had been WITH her mother the entire time that this had happened! There was no-one else upstairs at the time.

She questioned her mother who said, "ah don't mind her, its just the ghost she's very friendly and well-meaning." The girl who didn't believe in ghosts laughed it off and returned to her room, only to see the clothes once again folded and stacked neatly on the end of her bed. She threw them back in her case and told her Mother that she could not sleep in there and left to go back home.

Shortly before this, in the same pub, a gentleman had wondered in for a lunchtime drink, and asked the young woman at the bar for a beer. She stared blankly at him and didn't move, so he asked again, but once more there was no response from the barmaid. Astonished at the poor service he went to leave, at which time the landlady returned from the kitchen and said "oh I'm sorry I didn't hear you come in". The man explained what happened and said he had never seen such poor service and was leaving. The landlady replied – "but I'm the only one here my love". She then took him to the bar where the "barmaid" had mysteriously disappeared! The man, now shaken sat down with a complimentary brandy and has apparently never returned to the Swan.

Whilst I was there, I witnessed a very large old wooden door which was wedged open, shut in front of my very eyes. I examined it thoroughly and could see no reason for this door suddenly to swing shut in such a manner. I opened the door and walked through to call one of the other investigators and as I turned back around the door was once again open with the wedge firmly in place under it.

For a short period back in 2002, I was employed by Mentorn Television in London to help put together a pilot for a new paranormal show aimed at Channel 4. As part of my duties, I was sent out with a video camera to scout a number of potential spooky venues across the south of England, and I took Suzie Millar along to help me research each of the places.

Our first trip was to the Isle of Wight to look at Golden Hill Fort. This was a former army garrison with tales of a "smoking ghost".

As I walked around the disorienting building, I felt a presence of a large man following me, and sure enough a strong smell of tobacco. I turned around to film behind me and the fully charged camera battery suddenly failed on me. I asked Suzie to pass me the spare which was also fully charged, and sure enough as I connected it to the camera it read "battery full". I turned to where I had felt the presence to begin filming again and battery again failed with the display now again reading "battery empty". Apparently this is not the first time this had been reported at Golden Hill Fort. Many visitors had reported batteries dying suddenly in that area of the building.

Some time after my visit there, I read that a team had analyzed the tobacco smell at the fort and found it to be a type of tobacco that has not been sold for over 100 years!

Whilst on the Isle of Wight, we also visited an old disused mental asylum, which was very spooky and seemingly ideal for the show. Whilst there this burly builder came up to me and said "if you promise not to turn on the camera, I'll tell you about what happened to me here".

He was the owner of a demolition company that had been retained to knock down part of the building. He arrived to look over the building and was greeted by an old lady who told him he was in the wrong section of the building, and that he should go next door.

When he arrived next door, another woman said "no it's not this building it's the one next door" – he laughed and said but I've just been there and the old lady told me it was this one. The woman looked puzzled and walked back with him to the building next door….

You see you couldn't have been to this one she said, it's all boarded up and locked. The building was indeed locked and derelict, yet only minutes earlier it was open, with lights on and people walking around.

The woman led him back into the other building and showed him a number of photographs to see if he could identify the woman who spoke to him. After looking through a number of the photos he suddenly said "yes that's her". The woman enquired "are you quite sure?" Yes he replied. It turns out that the woman he had identified was a former patient of the establishment who had died there many years before.

No wonder he didn't want to go on camera and tell me his story!

Our next stop was a Napoleonic fort in the Solent just off Portsmouth. The only access was by boat, and a more isolated venue for the show I could not have found – yet it would also be ideal for the programme.

Suzie and I walked around the seagull-infested fort which was extremely spooky. Parts were extremely dark, lit only by our torches. Suddenly Suzie said "oh my God" I turned around saw something move behind her, it was a figure, human shaped but not solid. Suzie had also seen something move out of the corner of her eye.

My first thought was that there may be someone living in the fort, but then all of our batteries failed, both in the torches and in the video camera, we were suddenly standing in pitch darkness.

We decided to quickly make a move back to an area where there was at least some daylight, which wasn't easy when you can't see where you are going. Suddenly without any explainable reason, both torches came back on and the video was again reading "battery full". I have no rational explanation for what went on down there that day – but I certainly wasn't sorry to leave the place.

Our trip to the South had proved very fruitful in finding some ideal venues for the show, but after all that work it turned out that Channel 4 didn't take the programme.

Going back to one of my early trips to see Helen and Mike in Chepstow, I remember them taking me to a pub by a river for a drink. Graham Matthews was with us as was his then girlfriend Angie. It was here that I had my first really convincing encounter with my own clairvoyance gift.

I walked into the pub and said to Mike "busy in here isn't it" looking up into the air and NOT at the few living people in the pub. I noticed a woman in a long green Victorian style dress walking between two staircases in mid-air and pointed this out to Graham who immediately took a photograph. In the photo was a large glowing orb in the exact position I had shown him.

I then went to the bar and asked whether the pub was "haunted" and the woman behind the bar said yes and asked me why – and when I described the woman, the barmaid went pale and said, "my God – you've seen her"? Apparently the description was a perfect match to a ghost that had appeared on numerous occasions to staff and customers of the establishment.

This so intrigued the staff behind the bar, that one by one they came and sat with us and asked if I could do a "reading", something I had never attempted before. I said I would try but offered no guarantee. The first girl sat down and immediately I could see in my mind's eye, her as a child pushing a wheelbarrow full of freshly chopped logs up a long garden path. The house was situated in a remote area surrounded by fields and woodland. The man with her was her Grandfather who I named and described. As I opened my eyes, the girl had a tear in her eye as she said "how could you know that? I loved pushing my Granddad's wheelbarrow up to the house with logs in whenever I visited his secluded country house".

She went back to the bar where she told others of what I had said, and sure enough a steady stream of other staff members began asking me questions, all of whom I gave seemingly correct information to.

One in particular was the duty bar manager, who sat down with her arms crossed and said "ok then read me, I'm the biggest sceptic you will ever meet"… Now here was a challenge!

I closed my eyes and began to concentrate and suddenly got a girl's name, but the girl was not in spirit, but very much alive. She showed me a rash on her arms and told me it was Meningitis. I began to relay this information to the woman siting before me and told her that this was a niece who was 2 – 3 years old, and who she had nearly lost a short while before with the deadly virus. I described her and how she is now fully recovered. The woman looked at me and said "that's unbelievable – how do you do it?" I think she had expected me to say it was some kind of trick, but I was almost as shocked as she was as to how this was happening.

I still have no answer as to how these things suddenly happen, although I had been told by other clairvoyants, that I have "the gift of clairvoyance" many times in previous years. I do not promote myself as a Medium or clairvoyant, as I cannot seem to do it at will, but sometimes the information I get does seem uncannily accurate – and contains things that I could not have possibly known. Could I have been unwittingly tapping into the Universal Consciousness that I have spoken about before?

In another incident in the *Nth* Devon area, we were doing an investigation of a private house. We had been called in by the owner's son whilst she was away on holiday and had been asked not to make the address public, and I shall honour this by not pinpointing the town involved.

During a session in "circle" trying to establish what was in the house – I gave a description of a former neighbor who had since passed, who used to help with someone in a wheelchair who lived at the property. Once again the description of the person and events were correct. It was at this investigation however, that something far more curious took place.

Whilst asking questions in the circle, which was conducted in a downstairs living room, I had requested that any spirit present should knock once for yes and twice for no, but had received no audible response during the session. However, we later found that the knocks HAD been recorded in a bedroom upstairs on both sound recording devices AND on a video at the exact time of the session downstairs.

Could it have been that a time/space displacement had occurred and that the gauze or curtain between parallel dimensions had meant that the response was a short distance away from the place that the circle had taken place? This is certainly an area that requires a lot more experimentation, and I would advise any other investigators reading this book, to set up recording devices in other parts of the building whenever you conduct a circle or séance.

When the sceptics say that there is no real proof of the existence of the paranormal, or an "after-life" – they often expect the believers to provide such evidence in one night on an investigation, but for me, evidence has been something gained over a long period, ruling out coincidences and rational explanations to events. It's not so much a space flight – more a bicycle ride across the world.

Twenty One
UFO's Aliens & Abductions

Until I started presenting my radio programme Now THAT'S Weird, I had never really believed or thought too much about aliens, UFO's or abductions, but talking to some of my guests has really made me think again.

I have said on many occasions when relating to sceptics and cynics, that the "blind man CANNOT see – whereas the man with his eyes shut WILL not see". I guess I had to open my own eyes to see the evidence that sat there before me, so why should I so easily discount things that I hadn't seen or witnessed with my own eyes?

I suppose that it had always puzzled me as to why an alien may fly millions of light years across the Universes to simply leave a pretty pattern in a field, then fly home again.

What if however, that they were NOT flying across the Galaxy in spaceships, but were in fact transferring via stargate or from a parallel dimension much closer to us? Could this make aliens more believable?

What if aliens were NOT little green men from another planet – but ethereal type entities that we may confuse as ghosts, Sasquatch, goblins or fairies for example?

Or maybe, underground dwelling creatures that come from within the Earth's centre rather than from outside the planet? Maybe this could explain strange occurrences such as the Bermuda Triangle?

One of the guests on my radio show was Michael Mott – who has studied subterranean dwellers in depth, and within one hour of talking to him on the programme, he gave some very convincing arguments for why this may be the case. I would strongly suggest that you search for him on the Internet and read some of his work – it may also open your mind to a new way of thinking about alien life forms.

So what about abductions and cattle mutilations?

There has been little real hard evidence of abductions, but it seems strange that so many accounts of alleged abduction by aliens contain very similar accounts of operations, sexual practices and bright lights in the middle of the night. Can they all be having the same hallucinations? Seems very unlikely doesn't it?

If abductions DO take place, then why? What is there to gain by experimenting and toying with the human race in this way? Could it be to try to make hybrids for a dying race of aliens? Maybe it's for some kind of future invasion – but I am not easily convinced of this.

Many abductees claim to have had "implants" given to them whilst undergoing painful "surgery" at the hands of these alien entities, yet so far, no such implants have ever been found and identified as far as I am aware. But does the lack of proof mean they do not exist?

Animal mutilation is another area that has been labeled as the work of space traveling aliens, and it's true to say that there have been many cases that defy logical or rational explanation, but again a lack of real evidence to associate this with alien beings.

Many people have reported seeing bright lights in the sky, and many sightings have been reported from very credible witnesses such as airline pilots and Police Officers on duty – can they ALL be wrong?

A number of these sighting may well be due to the testing of secret military aircraft and "weather balloons" but these explanations cannot cover the greatest number of sightings.

SETI (The Search for Extra Terrestrial Intelligence) have for many years been attempting to gain messages from outer space – but has anyone attempted to communicate with the earth BELOW our feet? Beaming signals out into space is one thing, but we haven't finished exploring our own planet yet.

So for me, the answers just may lay here on earth and not in outer space.

Twenty Two
The Knights Templars - Another Quest?

Around 2002, many paranormal organizations around the world began documenting alleged "contact" with spirits of Knights Templars, and many began a quest to find out more about this legendary organization. I was one of those intrigued as to WHY the Knights Templars were coming up over and over again not only in investigations, but places I was drawn to visit were often built by or associated with the Templars.

History currently tells us that the Templars originated in France in the 11th century, but I am going to throw a spanner in the works here, after all, history has been documented incorrectly before.

It is my belief that the Knights Templars began in SCOTLAND in or around the 5th/6th century and were associated with the Culdee's in the Perth area. It is here that I began my search.

Strangely enough, it was in Rendlesham Forest that I channeled what turned out to be a longitude/latitude reference for an area close to Scone, home of the legendary "Stone of Scone".

Whilst in the Scone and Perth areas, I found evidence of a Scottish King Arthur, a Guinevere of the same time period in Perth, and stories of a "Round Table" in the same area. Could it be that the early Templars were in fact the original Knights of Arthur's Round Table thus bringing two great Grail legends together?

Obviously this is just a theory at this stage, but my research has provided me with enough intriguing information to continue my quest.

On a trip to Caithness in Scotland around the same time, I was shown Templar graves and was made aware of a Templar association with the Sinclair clan of Caithness. The Sinclair study Centre in Caithness provides evidence of this connection, and artifacts that firmly link the Knights Templars with Caithness and the Orkney Islands.

Indeed, it may well have been a Sinclair along with the Templars that made the very first discovery of the Americas long before Columbus.

In the 6th century, St. Columba is said to have brought Christianity from Ireland to the island of Iona, then onto mainland Scotland.

A Culdee group of holy men was then established at Scone, and as was told to me by a visitor guide at Scone Palace, it was on the Hill of Credulity at Scone that the Pictish King Nectan formally embraced the customs of the Church of Rome in 710. He also pointed out that the Moot Hill was already an important sacred site long before it was used for the crowning of the Kings of Scots.

Could it be that St. Columba and his holy leaders formulated the Knights Templar to protect the Culdee College and to seek the holy scrolls that Columba believed existed? Could it be that they visited the holy lands long before the first documented medieval crusades?

Many of the sites that I have earmarked for investigation in the Scone and Perth areas, point to the fact that Rosslyn Chapel may be a MAP and not the actual location of what was found and returned to Scotland. After all, Rosslyn was built hundreds of years later.

I have also found an association with the Templars and Loch Ness. It would seem that one of the strongest energy lines I have encountered, runs between Urquart Castle (a place visited by St. Columba) and Boleskine on the other side of the Loch, and I believe there to be Templar graves in Boleskine cemetery.

When Alastair Crowley chose Boleskine as a location for his attempts to contact his own guardian angel in a magical rite known as Abremalin, did he choose it because he too knew of these immense energies?

Historians tell us that the world "Templar" came from "Temple" as in Solomon's

Temple, but it is also means "TIME" – and as they always believed they would return in the future, could this have meant the "Knights of Time"?

Many Templar graves feature an egg-timer and the words "Momento Mori" which again has several meanings depending on the translation, but one such translation is "one moment more".

Templar gravestone with Momento Mori inscription.

Templars were usually buried close to Earth energy lines because they believed this made it easier to make the transition between this world and the next, and possibly back again. Therefore, the burials at Boleskine would make a lot of sense.

In America, a top researcher on Earth energies and grids, William Buehler, believes that the "round table" relates to the grid lines around the world, which provide these very energy lines. He believes that the site at Scone is a meeting place of several of these major grids, and the longitude and latitude details I gave him, were the exact pinpoint of this location. This seems more than a mere coincidence.

Could we once again be seeing a connection between Scotland, King Arthur and the Knights Templars?

The Sinclair connection continues in Scone, with one family member owning the very land on which my location is placed and I was told a short while ago that he has found something of "immense historical interest" on this land already but is unaware of just what it is that he may have in his possession.

There is a modern day Templar Order in Scotland (probably more than one) and I'm sure that much of what I am saying here will come as no surprise to some of the elders of that organization.

It has long been thought that a Templar army assisted the Scots in the Battle of Bannockburn, and turned an inevitable defeat into a memorable victory, adding yet more credence to a Scottish heritage for the Templars.

The historians will probably accuse me of having little firm evidence on which to build these foundations, but like the paranormal research I have done over the years, some things take a lot more explaining than just archeological digs. I am sure that in years to come, much more evidence WILL appear to support this theory. The Templars definitely made their presence felt across the world, and whilst many people search places such as Rennes Le Chateau in France, I find Templar history much nearer to home in places such as Temple Village in Cornwall, and at Bisham Abbey in Buckinghamshire to name but two ancient sites.

The Templars were also well documented in Newfoundland and through the America's a land that I believe they discovered with Sir Henry Sinclair.

The Sinclairs, formerly St. Clairs, were allegedly of Norman descent and appeared in Scotland around the 10th/11th centuries and it is at this time that the apparent link with the Knights Templars became apparent. The Orkneys meanwhile has a much stronger connection with the Vikings and other Scandinavian ancestors.

It is the Sinclair's that bear the main association with Rosslyn Chapel, and the apparent Knights Templar grave in the chapel is that of William Sinclair who it is claimed, was a member of the Templar Order.

Rosslyn is a very strange place, and many still believe that the Holy Grail or Ark of the Covenant are buried beneath its intricate brickworks, I however do NOT believe this. I do however, think that the inside of the chapel is a coded map which if ever deciphered, would lead to the discovery of at least some of the hidden holy artifacts.

If the Templars WERE at Scone before they were in France, and this was the birthplace of the order, then maybe here or even the ancient holy island of Iona, offers a far better choice of resting place or sanctuary for the artifacts. But what IS the Grail?

For many years, it was believed to be the goblet from the Last Supper, but more recent claims in books like The Holy Blood & The Holy Grail, and the fictional Da Vinci Code, theories have been put forward that the Holy Grail (from the original world Sangraal) is in fact the bloodline of Jesus Christ himself. Could this lead us back to the Sinclair's?

Whatever you believe, The Knights Templars figure in the story at some stage, and maybe the treasure they found was KNOWLEDGE.

Now I mentioned "stargates" a while ago – could these actually exist and be a way of traveling between points in space and time? If so, is THIS the knowledge that was hidden by the Templars – the Knights of Time? It seems far-fetched, but remember, we thought that the use of a mobile telephone device on the TV series Star Trek was far-fetched once.

What about the Ark of the Covenant? What immense powers may this box of secrets hold? Maybe the Templars also had the answer to this too. Maybe it was felt that the world was not ready for such knowledge at the time.

The quest of finding out more about the Knights Templar has taken me far beyond "ghost hunting" and into a realm of myth, legend and possible discovery – only time will tell whether my current theories are real or just my creative mind working overtime.

Twenty Three
Children & Sensitivity

I have long believed that children are all born with a sensitivity to spirit presence and on many occasions where they have an "invisible friend" they are actually communicating with a spirit child.

Society as it is today and has been for hundreds of years, brainwashes the child once they start to attend full time education and as such they are made to believe that they will be ridiculed if they believe in ghosts, aliens and other "taboo subjects" so the gift is eradicated over time.

Now if our souls and consciousness do in fact materialise our very thoughts, then in the same way, disbelief and negativity must also distinguish these entities.

It is my thought therefore, that to learn about the paranormal world around us, we must first UNLEARN all, we have been taught in these areas throughout our schooling.

My own youngest daughter Nikki, when very young, once told me that she used to talk to her Grandma Hemsworth every night before she went to sleep. This discovery came about when we heard her talking in bed one night, and between her words there was a period of silence as if listening to a reply and then indeed answering it.

She told me that Grandma Hemsworth who had passed a short time before) used to kiss her good night every single night, and always talked to her before she went to sleep. Now you could say she was imagining this but please first take the following into account:-

1) She barely KNEW her Grandma who died whilst she was still a baby, yet she relayed to us things about her that she could NOT have known.

2) We know now that we are closest to spirit contact during that period just before sleep.

3) My mother was very fond of my children and would have been devastated that she wasn't there to watch them grow.

Now let's just say for a moment that this was NOT a figment of Nikki's imagination, then perhaps as a naïve child she was just doing what comes naturally to every child prior to full time education.

My eldest daughter Leanne has always believed that she has seen spirits around our home and in other places and despite her Mother telling her not to believe "such rubbish" Leanne is still a complete believer based on her own experiences.

When my ex-wife's mother died, both Leanne and myself saw a mist appearing just a few minutes after the phone call from the hospital in front of a wardrobe in the master bedroom at our home in Dunstable. The room got unbelievably cold and Leanne calmly said "Dad is that Nan Bicknell over there"?

We all saw and felt the mist in front of the wardrobe and even my extremely skeptical ex-wife had to admit that it was "very strange".

I have had many cases sent to me by people who have experienced what they believe to be relatives appearing in photos at their children's birthday parties, including orbs around the child.

If it is true that children are sensitive, shouldn't these gifts be encouraged rather than ridiculed? After all, when you tell a child that they are being "stupid" every time they tell you they have seen something, then surely sooner or later they will stop telling you.

I am a firm believer in that children have great gifts which society denies them of over time and this is why so much of the ancient knowledge is now being lost.

If your child tells you that they have an invisible friend, or sees a dead relative, don't be so quick to dismiss it – take some photos around them, encourage them to ask questions of the person they are seeing and see if they can give you some information that THEY could not have known about the person – it just may amaze you.

Twenty Four
A United Paranormal Research World? Unlikely

There are thousands of paranormal organizations around the world, but very few ever work with or cooperate with each other, and I find this very unhelpful to research.

There seems to almost be a jealousy between many organizations – especially towards those that have appeared on TV like Phantom or Fraud – yet surely we are all trying to establish the same thing – proof one way or the other as to what causes paranormal phenomena?

Over the years, there have been numerous attempts for "alliances" between groups but few have ever existed beyond a few months after arguments begin over the way it should be run or administered.

I would like to see all the major groups that do proper scientific research, put forward their research results to a major non-profit organization that publishes these results together with information of research that produces similar results from varying groups.

It is only THIS way that we can really survey just how many "facts" there are in paranormal research, and how much coincidence exists.

One group alone working on an experiment can produce some good results, but how much more believable would it be if 50 unconnected organizations were getting similar results to the same type of experiments? Perhaps then, people who are skeptical or "on the fence" may take the results far more seriously.

Some organizations are led by people who have been known to "cheat" their information results, or make up research papers, and these people should be barred from taking part in this overseen and jointly presented alliance.

It should also become commonplace that all organizations in the alliance should have significant insurance cover when doing an investigation to protect themselves and the venues against damage, accidents and fires etc. After all, what would YOU do if the National Trust or another such body, rang you the day after an investigation and said they were suing you for millions of pounds because one of your team scribbled a moustache on one of their prized Picassos?

There would be many other advantages of having a worldwide alliance of paranormal groups such as:-

1)   Cheaper negotiated insurance rates
2)   An access to worldwide media releases
3)   Internal newsletters
4)   Updates of new breakthroughs and equipment available
5)   Negotiated specialist rates for purchase of things like EMF meters and other gadgets
6)   A worldwide log of investigators in areas you may be investigating
7)   A chance to share information between groups
8)   Set experiments for us all to try under governed conditions
9)   An agreed deal for alliance with venues to stop "over charging" and to stop unprofessional groups from accessing and "ruining" relationships with venues

These are just a few of the obvious advantages of such an organization, and I for one would give it my full and hearty support if correctly set up and administered.

Have YOU had experience working within such an alliance? Whether good or bad let me know how it worked for you and what the benefits and downsides were. E-mail: ross@phantomorfraud.org.

Twenty Five
The Hitchhiker's Guide to Haunting!

Let's have a quick and humorous look at how some organizations conduct investigations.

One of the first stake-outs I ever attended saw half a dozen enthusiasts camped out in a dark damp derelict building with torches and note pads sitting on the floor for hours at a time waiting for Fred the ectoplasm to walk through a wall, shake their hand and say "Hi I'm Fred and I'm dead"!

It really can be quite disappointing if you sit for days and nights waiting for the full body entity to come and shake your hand. Without results, you can see your group dissipate quite quickly.

I have also seen people walking around with EMF meters wondering why they are all going off so frequently and boasting that "this is the most haunted house I have ever been in" – but wait a minute – if an EMF meter is not set correctly, doesn't it go off the minute it is moved? Therefore walking around with it may not be the way to use the equipment.

I have also witnessed investigators becoming bored because they have been allocated to the same spot for hours and are becoming fidgety, so they then begin talking about their week, telling each other jokes and completely missing the entity who has just walked passed them (probably laughing its head off). OBSERVATION is one of the most important parts of a stake-out – so make sure your team does not spend more than 45 – 60 minutes in one location and give them regular breaks to talk and "lighten up". You'll be amazed at the difference this makes.

On my investigations, much laughter and joviality takes place during breaks – in my experience spirits like laughter and it encourages more results whilst also allowing your team to let off steam between sections of the investigation.

The color spectrum – do YOU know how to separate infrared from ultra-violet, does your equipment include a good mix of Polaroid, digital, 35 mm and infrared photography equipment? Do you fully understand how to use night vision camera equipment?

These areas are so important if you wish to distinguish between "orbs" and dust etc. and to see if you have any real "paranormal activity" in your pictures.

Do you study your video frame by frame? I once found a body shaped shadow moving across a staircase which couldn't be seen in normal "play mode". We only saw it in frame by frame or in fast forward search/fast reverse search. It was established that this entity may have moved in "temporal time" – a speed outside of that in which any human can more.

Have you looked in windows and mirrors in your photographs for faces or images?

Have you ever checked to see if there are more people in your picture than were in the room at the time?

We all tend to look for orbs or strange flashes in the photographs, whilst missing the REAL paranormal, images that are in the picture.

EVP's (electro voice phenomena) – do you use different kinds of recording devices, such as an old flat-deck cassette recorder with multi directional microphone, a digital dictation device, a mini disk digital sound recorder? You may find that some devices capture more than others – but only by using ALL of them on your investigations will you discover this.

Do you just put the recorders out and hope for the best or do you ASK spirit to record something for you? After all, good manners and asking the question of your guests might just be the difference between getting or not getting a good EVP.

There is great free software you can download from the Internet called Audacity which you can find with a simple Google search. This software allows you to look at the EVP's on the PC, check the waveform for differences in level, frequency etc, and it also allows you to clean up the sound.

I used Audacity when making the DVD – The Dead Are Talking and found certain files were NOT saying what we had thought. For instance one EVP was brought to me as saying "Not essential" but when we cleaned it up on Audacity it actually said "John to Central" – obviously a case of a freak radio wave from a taxi company!

You must ALWAYS rule out all rational and logical explanations before putting forward your "paranormal evidence" or you will just be laughed out of existence by the sceptics. Do not allow them such an easy answer to your evidence!

Many paranormal groups accept virtually anyone who applies for membership but if you check them carefully they may already have been expelled from a number of other groups. I once had a guy say to me "can't you stop all this scientific nonsense – I just want a laugh on a Saturday night chasing ghosts" – would you want an idiot like him on your team?

There are also a number of people who are urgently seeking a social life, and will end up bedding half your investigators – not much evidence of the paranormal will be captured by these people who are always far too busy investigating the under garments of other investigators.

Mr. and Mrs. Unreliable are also a problem within paranormal circles, promising to be at a stake-out and then letting you down constantly at the last minute – you do not want to waste your time with people such as this and again you will often find other groups have already gotten rid of them – so ask around when deciding on a new member application.

Clairvoyants – it is my opinion that there are far more "poor ones" than there are good ones and again other groups may well advise on who they have had success with. Do not use mediums who want to charge ridiculous fees as most good ones will either do it for nothing or for their travel/accommodation costs as they too wish to prove soul survival.

Use the clairvoyant sensibly not just for holding a "séance". Do not tell them what venue you are attending – meet them in a pre-arranged location some miles from the venue and then let them walk around the building and see what they pick up – it may give you a far better understanding of the building and its history and where to best situate your cameras.

In areas where you know a lot of visual activity has been witnessed, lock off a camera, set an EMF meter and some control objects such as a marble and a ball, and keep your investigators away from the area – watch the area from a control room – you may get far better results.

Don't believe everything you see on TV!!!! Many paranormal shows are on entertainment channels and they have to provide such entertainment for viewers so they are not always true accounts of what actually happened. I was lucky in that Ghost Detectives went out on a documentary factual channel and we were not expected to "cheat" in any way. What happened was real and nothing was faked.

Beware of "reputations". Certain well documented "haunted castles, manors and houses" have a reputation that provides a healthy income from tourists and ghost groups, but they are not always the best places for your investigation. Usually these venues will also want a sizeable fee from your group. I always personally find that little known hauntings in private homes produce far more interesting investigations as there is usually nothing known about the venue so there is no opportunity for advanced research.

Membership fees are a good way of getting a little income for your organization, but this can also cause problems if you are not doing regular investigations. We found we were getting complaints from people when we were charging membership fees as it is not always possible to have regular investigations if you don't have venues or are busy at certain times with other things. We have now ceased charging membership to Phantom or Fraud.

You can make merchandise available, but again we were accused by the troublesome minority of being "in it for the money" and "making money from the paranormal" when we tried this – it seems again, that people in the paranormal community resent anyone who covers theirs costs! I have personally invested probably in the region of £50,000 in equipment and investigations and doubt I have made 10% of that back through membership and merchandise! I am in it for TRUTH, for ANSWERS and for the quest to prove or disprove the question of life after death and along the way it would be nice to break even occasionally but if I was in it for the money, I would have chosen a far easier trade and one with less cynics and nasty attacking people involved.

Be careful who you trust in paranormal circles, as my personal experience shows that very few of them are really your friends – many are just out to use and abuse, so choose your friends and confidants wisely. Also, you should remember a very well known phrase:-

"Keep your friends close but your enemies even closer".

Your web site is your best friend in paranormal research, here you can post what you want the world to see, whilst keeping certain information for the eyes of your members only through password protected forums and members pages. You can also set up an online shop where you can take money from any merchandise or membership fees you care to charge to help you fund your research and investigations. Here you can also promote your organization to potential new members.

I do still run paranormal training weekends so please feel free to contact me if you wish to come on one of these as they are a great way of setting up your own organization.

Ghost Tours – you may find these a great way of getting to have a look at reputedly haunted sites for a small fee before deciding on an investigation. Some are very good and give you access to areas you would not otherwise be able to get to, but others are very limited and do not even allow you take photo's so please check before spending your money.

Haunting Breaks do some great weekends in haunted places and you can find out more about them at www.hauntingbreaks.co.uk

It is always wise to read up on other people's experiences in venues which you can find on many organization websites via a Google search of the venue name. This way "dead duck venues" can be seen in order that you don't waste valuable time or money going there. It is also good to read books by authors like Peter Underwood and John L. Spencer who are serious investigators who will tell you of their own experiences.

Keep all your old video tapes until you have viewed them properly including frame by frame searches as it is all too easy when money is tight, to use old video tapes rather than splash out on new ones, but you may just tape over that Holy Grail of videos – the full entity paranormal clip!

Back up all your photographs – as PC's do crash from time to time and digital photographs can all be lost. Do the same with your EVP recordings – you never know when you may need them.

Keep written records of ALL your investigations whilst they are still clear in your mind – and again BACK THEM UP to archive CD Roms.

Remember that if you are taking a lot of equipment into a venue, you may disturb the energies already there, so why not plan your investigation over a long weekend or for a week, as few one night investigation provide good evidence, and if you keep getting no results your team will eventually lose interest and your organization will collapse.

Do not confine yourself to "ghost hunting". Remember that the world of the paranormal covers a wide range of phenomena and by restricting yourself to just awaiting the arrival of the "full body entity" you may miss something far more important to your research.

Schedule days off! It is essential when doing longer term investigations that your team get days off or at least time away from the venue to relax and unwind, and thus bond together socially as a team.

Try to have your team working in groups of three or four as follows:-

1) With video camera/night vision
2) With stills camera
3) With note pad, pen and torch
4) With EMF meter, temperature gauge etc.

This will allow for evidence of alleged paranormal activity by more than one person thus substantiating the sighting, and can also corroborate the activity by capturing various forms of evidence.

Be very careful of "publicity seekers". I have come across many pub landlords and other venue owners who will "manufacture evidence" to get your group in and then get all the local press and radio reporters in to get publicity for their venue in the hope it will increase custom.

Check out for geographic fault lines, known energy lines and reported "ley lines" in the area of the venue, as these may have a bearing on your planned stake-out.

What was on the site BEFORE the current property? It may be that a fairly modern property may sit on the former site of something far more interesting such as an asylum, prison, graveyard or site of a murder etc. Not all alleged hauntings are to do with the current property.

Be willing to travel – after all there are some great reported hauntings in other counties and other countries. For instance if a "poltergeist" is reported as being active this may only last for a few weeks – be prepared to travel with your team if such is reported and keep a fund for these specific short notice assignments.

Transportation – this is VERY important as you will probably start to accumulate a lot of equipment so an estate car or van will be a necessity after a while so if you are starting off in paranormal research and are also looking for a new vehicle at the time, make sure you think this through.

Try to allocate teams to stake-outs based on their expertise so that you have a good mix of personnel to include photographers, cameramen, sceptics (or at least open minded rational thinkers) good team leaders, people with strong observational skills etc.

Testing observation is fairly easy. When taking your team members out on a social event such as a visit to the local pub, have someone planned to walk in and talk to you then leave the bar area, returning after an hour or so. Shortly before their return ask everyone if they recall someone coming in to see you, and if so was it a male or female, what were they wearing (in detail) what were they talking to you about – what time did they arrive/leave etc? It will help prove to you who has the strongest observational skills in your group and will also trigger the memories of others.

When installing cameras in venues and running them back to a control area, remember to keep the wires safe so that people cannot trip over them. This is best done by using gaffer tape to secure wires in walkways etc. – but again be sure to remember that gaffer tape in certain circumstances, may leave marks or take off loose paint work – so be careful.

Allocate members of your team to setting up cameras and control rooms – if they all know their specific jobs and do them regularly, the set up and dismantling process will be far quicker on stakeouts.

If you have "pretty and flirty" girls on your team – it is a good idea to ask them to "dress down" on investigations as they can be quite a distraction!

When negotiating an investigation with a property owner/manager be sure to make him/her fully aware of what the investigation entails, as there is nothing worse than hearing a few minutes before you begin that you cannot access certain rooms because he has "guests staying" or you have to be finished by midnight. (And yes it DOES happen.)

Pubs are the worst for this, as many are busy until midnight, and many areas cannot be accessed until the pub closes, they will then often lock up the bar and cellar areas where you may have found some of your best evidence.

Those with accommodation, may have areas with guests staying where you have to be extremely quiet and again you cannot guarantee this during an investigation.

Proper planning can avoid these problems.

SAFETY – this is a VERY important issue. Never allow your team to be in an unsafe environment without supervision. This can include derelict buildings where floors may be unsafe, drug users may be using the premises, roof area may be collapsing, squatters may be present, etc.

Always try to have a "first aider" on your investigation to deal with minor injuries.

Be sure to have the contact phone numbers of the owner (if he or she is not staying with you on the investigation) in case alarms go off in the night, or fuses blow, etc.

Physical injury is not your only worry on a stake-out – many people suffer psychological damage from experiences in a "haunted house" and on occasions you could be sued for such injury if you have not taken the correct precautions to safeguard your team. If someone is becoming agitated – get them out straight away, get them a glass of water and take them into a lighted or "safe area" and talk them through the problem. Don't just hope the problem will go away.

ALWAYS look for the rational or logical explanation before claiming it is paranormal. If a door suddenly slams, check to see if someone didn't do it or whether there was a draft. If something moves "on its own" check to see if the floor is level – it may LOOK level but few floors actually are in older buildings.

Brief your team on the safety rules and regulations and the do's and don'ts of the stakeout BEFORE you begin.

Always respect the venues request for anonymity or "no publicity" if requested.

These are just a few guide points but ones I hope you will find useful.

Twenty Six
Physical Mediumship

Physical or materialization mediums, have fascinated me for some years, with very few actual examples of good mediums seeming to exist, and a lot of bad publicity surrounding the famous physical mediums of the past.

I wrote to the now defunct "Noah's Ark Society" some time ago asking for their help in trying to examine and experiment with current working physical mediums, but ended up only being attacked by the organization for my approach. Their web site said they actively "promoted physical mediumship" but when approached, the doors closed and I was torn apart on their web site for wanting to work with them. I have to say I wasn't unhappy when the organization collapsed.

What came out of the ruins of the NAS was The Zerdin Fellowship, with many of the same members but under new management – a far more friendly and approachable organization and an acceptance of my ideas to run more scientific experiments to see whether there was any truth to the idea that these mediums can manifest an actual physical apparition seemingly at will.

However, it seems that only TWO working physical mediums exist within their membership, one in Australia and one that didn't appear too keen to be put forward at this stage. The others were "in development" apparently – so another dead end.

It was then that I met Patrick McNamara and Marion Dampiere-Jeans through guests on my radio show, and thought that if both claimed to be physical mediums, we should try to get them working together. They both seemed delighted at the idea of working together and with Proof or Fraud to try to promote physical mediumship to the world. No restrictions on where they worked, no banning of cameras their physical séances, no copyright restrictions on any images captured and a willingness to undergo scientific enquiry.

On Saturday April 29th, 2006, we brought them both together at the George & Dragon Hotel in West Wycombe in Buckinghamshire together with members of my team Nita Grant, Mark and Jocelyn Brinsden, Penny Dando and Gary Johnson.

On arrival the day before, Patrick and his associate Karl, walked around the building and immediately announced that it was amongst the 5 most haunted places he had ever visited and felt confident of a successful physical séance to take place the following night.

On the night of the event, room 10 of the hotel was chosen for the circle (a sitting of the clairvoyant team) and all the equipment was taken to the room to set up. The room was lit with small red and blue lights and four video cameras were positioned in the four corners of the room, with a fifth outside the room. EVP recorders were setup at various points around the room.

Two of the cameras were BVS (Beyond the Visible Spectrum) mini-cams lit by "black light devices" a brand new area of infrared technology never before used in a physical séance situation. These cameras give broadcast quality black and white images in pitch darkness, unlike its more grainy brother the "night vision/infrared" camera.

A "cabinet" was set up around the entrance to the bathroom door for "spirit to develop energy".

On a table in the centre of the room was a trumpet shaped instrument which Patrick told us would probably be the centre of spirit attention.

We all took our seats in the circle at just after midnight and Patrick McNamara got things started with a prayer for protection.

Within minutes messages started to come through mediums sitting in the circle, including some very well known names who were supposedly present including Arthur Conan Doyle, Tennyson, Louis Armstrong and Leslie Flint. I myself was also bringing names through and correctly identified people known only to Patrick and also one of his known spirit guides with the unusual name of Janus.

Patrick begin to show us examples of mists and flashing sparks of light which he referred to as "photoplasm". He explained that spirits were now trying to move away from the dangerous practice of using "ectoplasm" which can make mediums very ill, and that photoplasm was the future of the physical séance.

Most of us were aware of major changes to the atmosphere in the room, and the change of energies and temperatures around us but as yet no physical appearances of spirit.

Nita Grant then mentioned that there was something mischievous present and that if we wanted to see more actually physical movement it may be a good idea to encourage it to come forward, something that Karl and Patrick were not keen on.

Almost immediately, Gary Johnson appeared to become very distressed and began jerking and choking, and then announced he was Thomas Edison. No sooner had he done this than he began jerking and choking again and then announced in his own voice that his spirit guide had attempted to stop the spirit entering his body and had rejected it. Both myself and Patrick agreed that this was not Edison but a mischievous imposter.

Again Gary began to choke and jerk, and Marion who was sitting next to him, began to stroke his back and encourage the spirit to leave.

Things then began to calm down again within the circle and Patrick announced that by inviting a mischievous spirit into the circle was the wrong thing to do and has manifested the entity.

We then became aware of the trumpet in the centre of the table starting to move slightly something that most of those present witnessed. There were also small sparks of light near its base.

Throughout the séance Patrick demonstrated lines of photoplasm that we could see quite clearly and that appeared to come from the ends of our fingers when we ran them through these areas of subtle energy.

I must admit – I had received a message myself in the weeks prior to the experiment, that we may experience new ways of contact by spirit during this circle. I also was told that spirit are working on new ways of talking in circle without using a medium's voice box and thus causing less problems to the medium's present.

Whilst no physical apparitions actually appeared, there were definitely strange things happening in that room, and things that we were all aware of, and it is my belief that this was the first of many such experiments with this team of people, that would eventually develop into a very strong physical circle.

I believe that by continuing this work in more depth and more regularly with Patrick, Karl and Marion at the helm, we will eventually be given more and more evidence of soul survival.

Twenty Seven
The Church & Its Effect on Us

Now here I aim to be a little controversial and may well upset quite a few people but I feel it needs to be said.

Let me start by saying that I am a believer in a creator God figure, but feel I can talk adequately to him on a one to one basis ANYWHERE, I do not need to attend a building full of rule-makers, hypocrites and Sunday hymn-singers to make contact.

My own experiences of churches are that they make the rules up as they go along to "police the masses" , they invented the "devil and hell" for the very same reason, they told us what gospels we should and shouldn't read, and changed the original sacred texts to suit their own rulings.

Lets take one example "Let not the WITCH live" which in its original Hebrew was "let not the POISONER live" – and whilst there is a great similarity between those two words in Hebrew, the translation was no error.

We now know that the gospel of Thomas and the more recently discovered Gospel of Judas – tell very different stories form that which the church wanted us to see – and when the bible was compiled it was decided to call these gospels "heretic" and therefore not to include them in the good book. This was not a decision made by God or Jesus as far as we are aware.

For many years it has been rumored that documents exist within the vaults of the Vatican and other places that would destroy the very foundations of the Catholic religion – so why are we not allowed to see them?

In the churches we are told we are not allowed to commit sins – yet many church goers are exposed regularly as doing one thing and saying another. Wasn't Jesus quoted as saying "let he who is without sin cast the first stone"?

Roman Catholic priests we are told, have the power to forgive sins by giving out a series of "Hail Mary's" – but does any man on Earth REALLY have that power – I think not. We'd all love to believe that we can have our sins so easily forgiven but I doubt that it would stand for very much come judgment day. Can you imagine the conversation at the "pearly gates" going something like – "oh yes that's true St. Peter I did kill a few people, slept around with all my neighbors and stole the Crown Jewels, but it's all ok now because I was forgiven by my local priest". Perhaps we should all be fitted with "Hail Mary meters".

Other religions fair no better belting out all the do's and don'ts from a book that they themselves know bears little resemblance to the original sacred texts.

What about Islam? Every day we hear how the rest of us are "infidels" because we don't happen to sing from their particular hymn book and they regularly issue Fatwah's against those that dare to criticize what they say – I expect they'll issue one against me after this.

Terrorists from the Islamic faith claim to be martyrs and truly believe that they will go straight to heaven when they kill innocent people with their bombs and attacks – how can these people be given the keys to heaven?

So is it time for a new form of religion?

Well perhaps more so an "old style of religion" that of communication with spirit directly and not through the usual known channels. Perhaps the outlawing of Pagan religions by the churches was for the very reason that they were scared of them, knowing that perhaps they had far more chance of people following them than the churches?

Let's look at one phrase allegedly from the original sacred scripts:

"In my father's house there are many mansions" – supposedly said by Jesus himself. Could he have been referring to the many dimensions I have spoken about here in this book?

Another term "beware of familiar spirits" – maybe we could compare this to the mischievous spirit at the physical séance who pretended to be Thomas Edison?

Now I have long said that if we PROVE soul survival we will indeed prove a lot of what is written in the sacred texts to be true, and the ascension of Christ to be the rising spirit that we now believe to be possible from all human beings at the end of our physical life here on earth. So be this the case, why does the church continue to denounce those of us involved in paranormal research? Would it not HELP their cause?

There is far more evidence for soul survival through paranormal research, than there is for much of what the church preaches, but the church leaders tell us we must have FAITH and evidence to support it would not be allowed. Any ideas why? It defies me.

As I said, I believe in a God creator, I believe in life after death, and I believe we can all talk to him on request – so why the church?

I have said it before and I will say it again "the worse thing that ever happened to Christianity – was Christians"!

Perhaps we should just all look to become more spiritual – and develop our own spirituality and contact with our creator?

We can all freely access the religious writing of varying cultures and make our own minds up on what we wish to believe and what we wish to discount. Why only recently I saw a documentary about whether "Jesus Christ" actually died on the cross or whether he survived and went to live out his days in Kashmir!

Who knows what is the truth and what is the creation of others along the way. After all, rumors start with "bring three and four pence we're going to a dance" and end up as "bring reinforcements we're going to advance!"

Twenty Eight
The End of the World is Nigh!
Not Bloody Likely!

Since as far back as we can remember, man has been predicting the end of the world, the most recent having been the turn of the century. Many people thought that our goose was cooked on December 31st 1999 – but surprise, surprise – most of us woke up as usual on January 1st 2000!

Sooth-Sayers, "wise men" and precognitives have all given dates for the end of the world, from Nostradamus to the Mayan elders, but why DOES man have this seeming fascination with the end times?

Again we look to the bible and the end time prophecies, and what the bible refers to as "the rapture". Has man been brainwashed into believing that we are all doomed?

Let's take a look at the Mayan predictions. The Mayan calendar ends on December 23rd 2012 and many believe that because previous Mayan predictions have been so accurate, this is the date we must all consider with fear and dread. However if you study it a little more carefully, you may find it actually says "a new beginning" rather than the end! Perhaps we are therefore, entering a far more spiritual age ahead?

I have been told by numerous clairvoyants, that we are heading for an end to the "physical world" and moving into a more spiritual and ethereal existence. Could this be part of the big change that is happening around the world right now?

There is a belief that everything in our physical world has a vibration, and that if you can adjust your vibration you can even walk through a brick wall – indeed I know at least three people who say they have done it. All of these people are sane, ordinary folk whom give me no reason to disbelieve what they say.

So lets say for a moment, that nothing is quite as it seems and that we are actually living in a world where nothing is actually physical and is all in fact an illusion – could your brain cope with understanding that? Mine certainly couldn't – but maybe its because we all use our BRAINS when we should be using our minds more?

The human brain is like the workings of a PC – it does the job it needs to do to control its machine – the human body – but it cannot possibly cope with wonders of the universe which are well beyond its understanding and capability. But lets say the brain connects to the mind in the same way as your PC connects to external servers and the Internet – maybe this WAY we CAN understand more and ourselves tap into the universal consciousness or knowledge?

Have you ever pondered with that brain-numbing equation of what is at the end of space? We know its infinite but our brain wants a conclusion, so we see a brick wall as the end, but then the brain says yes but what is AFTER the brick wall, because that does not have infinite thickness? When you try to ponder this it is no wonder why there is such a fine line between brilliance and insanity. It poses a potential brain overload.

Now many of us search for our answers through paranormal research, biblical writings, history, etc. – but maybe we should look INSIDE not outside for these answers?

If indeed the world IS going to end, and I'm sure it will one day (hopefully not in the too near future) then maybe we already know the answers but just don't know how to access that particular "server" within our consciousness?

Going back to the Mayan prediction, I have always believed that the date 12.23.2012 has a special significance but then again I suppose you could say the same about 11.11.2011. But WHY did the Mayans stop counting two days before Christmas in 2012?

Like many cultures, they studied astronomy and made most of their predictions around the alignments of the stars, but how could they have been so accurate with their predictions when our own modern day astronomers still can't get it right?

What about the "day of judgment"? Could it be true that we will all be judged by the creator in the end of days? If so will we pay for the misdemeanors of our long dead ancestors who aren't there to be judged for themselves? Or WILL they be there in spirit?

Perhaps we ARE our ancestors, it could be that the same souls do the rounds and we are all constantly reincarnated.

So if the end of the world IS nigh – what might happen? Could it be a massive meteor storm? Maybe an alien attack? How about a nuclear war or two? Perhaps even the sun going out? But maybe the answer is a lot simpler – such as man's own creations like computers killing us all? Maybe avian flu will wipe us out? Or perhaps man will invent the very virus that kills us all as a chemical weapon? Maybe we ARE our own killers?

We have been destroying the planet we live on for centuries, probably in the past few decades more than ever before, and whilst we now all know about the "hole in the ozone" and "global warming" the greatest majority of the population really don't believe it will bother them in their lifetime.

Perhaps now is the time for all of us to take a step back, think and try to make some positive changes before it really IS too late.

Twenty Nine
Working Towards a New Future for Paranormal Research

It has taken many years to get science and medicine to sit up and take notice of the paranormal as a genuine area of research, but I'm glad to say that this is now finally happening.

We are finally starting to see scientists and doctors admitting that some things DEFY rational and logical explanation and thus need further investigation. Great thinkers like Professor J.J. Hurtak, Professor Gary Schwartz and Dr. Sam Parnia are a new breed who realize that there may well be a lot more to the universe than was previously thought and at last – our area of investigation is being taken a little more seriously.

We are currently hearing of the "string theory" which seems to give evidence of parallel dimensions existing – they just can't yet figure out how many.

We are also hearing that something DOES seem to leave the body at the point of death and move on elsewhere.

We are also hearing of evidence to support the fact that the mind is very different from the brain. I knew that years ago guys – do try and keep up!

We are now hearing of more and more success with alternative healing remedies – potions and organic items that have been around for thousands of years – although senior members of the medical establishments still call it no more than the "placebo effect". However if the placebo effect works – then surely that proves an even greater discovery – we can heal ourselves with belief!

In 1999 I met a healer who told me that if I just believed strongly enough that I would never get a cold or a sore throat – I wouldn't get them. Since then I have NEVER had a cold or sore throat! My kids used to bring bugs home from school all the time and everyone around me caught them except me.

Whilst filming Ghost Detectives, we were on location in Cornwall at Pengersick Castle and I woke up feeling very dizzy and unable to get out of bed without falling over (and no I hadn't been on the beer). Suzie Millar gathered the troops to assist me and it was decided to call in a doctor as my "temperature was very high". I said no just leave me to get rid of it myself – but they insisted.

A doctor arrived and diagnosed acute tonsillitis and said I would probably be bed-ridden for a week and certainly unable to talk or work. He prescribed antibiotics which a member of the team went and got for me, and it was decided that Andy Matthews would take over my role as Associate Producer of filming. They all left the hotel to go to the castle at around 11:30 a.m. By 3:00 p.m. I was sitting downstairs talking to the hotel owner and by 5:00 p.m. I was on site continuing my job – fully recovered and WITHOUT any of the antibiotics.

So I believe that we all DO have the ability to heal ourselves, if we just have enough faith in our own incredible abilities.

So what about the future…..

Imagine a world, where life after death is PROVEN conclusively and we all know that we will exist beyond our physical form. It would certainly change the way we live, and the way we see our friends and family when they pass away. Perhaps we would be more open to accepting them back in their ethereal bodies?

What about medicine? Will the knowledge that we CAN heal ourselves, see an eventual end to the major pharmaceutical companies that seem to control so much of the world's money, health and day to day activities?

What about those cynics and skeptics who have to eat all of their own words? Hope I'm still around to see THAT one!

In the nearer future though, it would be nice to think that the work of myself and others have at least opened the eyes of many more people, and finally achieved the attention of science and medicine.

What we need now, are more inventions to test things like Earth energies and spirit presences, more defined cameras in the infrared and ultra-violet spectrums and a real investment in the research of all things paranormal.

We also need the larger paranormal groups to start working closer together with a series of set experiments to make some firm conclusions from the research we have all done to date. Only then can we prove what many of us believe we already know.

I would ask all of you who read this book, to try six experiments for me on an on-going basis, and report the results back to me via e-mail at ross@phantomorfraud.org.

1) Keep a digital camera nearby you at all times and whenever you think you see something move out of the corner of your eye, take several photographs of the area, and see if anything unusual appears in it.

2) Whenever you feel a cold or a sore throat coming on, keep telling yourself "I do not GET colds and sore throats" – do not take any medicine of any kind for 24 hours and keep busy to keep your mind off the symptoms. See if it disappears on its own.

3) Before you go to bed at night once a week, put a Dictaphone out or a cassette recorder and ask any spirit present to leave a message of some kind for you – it sounds nuts but you may just be surprised.

4) Do regular PSI tests with your family, especially young children. Make two sets of six identical cards up with various shapes on such as a circle, a triangle, a square, a rectangle, a pyramid and a wavy line. Sit yourself and the other family member at different sides of the room back to back and have a third person act as a witness. Choose who will be the "receiver" and who will be the "sender". The sender should then concentrate hard on the image and picture the other person in their minds eye looking at it. The sender should then hold up the card so that only the witness can see it. The "receiver" should then also do the same, and see how many you get right.

5) Write down what you would like to dream about, and leave the note by the side of your bed before you go to sleep. If in the morning you HAD that dream, note the results, and see how many times this works over the course of a month.

6) Try to make yourself a pair of dowsing rods from old wire coat hangers by bending them into an L shape. Then ask a family member to hide a pound coin in a room. When they have hidden it, enter the room with the rods in front of you held about a foot apart. Walk slowly forward and ask the rods where the pound coin is.

Once you have done one or more of these experiments over a 4-week period, please send me your results.

E-mail ross@phantomorfraud.org or by post to Ross Hemsworth c/o Reality Press, P.O. Box 91, Foresthill, CA 95631.

Thirty
The Guests on My Radio Show Who Have Opened My Mind

I have been extremely lucky that my weekly radio show has brought me into contact with some incredible people researching all kinds of paranormal related subject matter, and whilst I cannot name them all, this chapter will outline some of the guests that have had a lasting effect on my life.

I must start with the very first guests on Show 1 back in September 2005, Professors J.J. and Desiree Hurtak. The Hurtaks have become good friends of mine over the past couple of years and I was delighted that they offered to be my first guests on the new show when it launched.

Professor J.J. Hurtak is at the very forefront of scientific research into what many may label "strange phenomena". He is an Egyptologist, Anthropologist, expert of Mayan and Aztec history and writer of the world famous Keys of Enoch, a book that it is said is in every world leader's collection. He spoke at the World Summit in Johannasburg recently in front of world leaders including George Bush and Tony Blair, and is one of the most brilliant minds it has ever been my pleasure to meet.

The Hurtak's spent a whole day and evening with my team in Berkshire a while back, answering their questions and talking about their own work and research. They accompanied us on a trip to the "Hellfire Caves" in West Wycombe and then joined us for an evening meal – it was a day that I will never forget.

On the radio show – they discussed their research into "alta-terrestrials" one step beyond "extra-terrestrials" and explained the changes that are happening all around us right now. I can honestly say – that as scientists and great thinkers – EVERYONE should attend their seminars if ever you get the opportunity.

David Icke – Many people only remember David because of all the adverse publicity surrounding his alleged claims of being the "son of God" – but hey, aren't we ALL sons and daughters of God?

David has been on my show a couple of times now, and each time I get flooded with e-mails saying things like "he actually makes a lot of sense" and "this guy has the real truth at his fingertips"! Perhaps we should forget the adverse publicity and listen to what he has to say, as so much of it makes sense in today's world.

OK – so I'm still not personally convinced that the Royal Family regularly turn into lizards – but then having seen so many strange things in my life, who am I to say it isn't possible? But his thoughts on the Illuminati families that run our world – make an awful lot of sense to me. He also showed me that some of the large pharmaceutical companies maybe letting have us all have access to chemicals that could be very bad for us – and they are all so very powerful that no-one can stop them.

I would strongly suggest that you all take a closer look into David's work – and whilst no-one has ALL the answers, remember that each holds a piece of the jigsaw, and it is for you to take out the information that you believe to be correct and important.

The Reverend Lionel Fanthorpe – as an ordained Priest and a paranormal researcher, Lionel treads where other church ministers fear to go – but as a black-belt in martial arts would YOU argue with him? He rides a Harley Davidson motorcycle and is probably best known for presenting TV series' such as Fortean TV and Bloody Towers.

Lionel was a fantastic guest and really does have his finger on the pulse in matters of ghost research and UFO's as head of BUFORA. He keeps an open mind on most subjects and believes without doubt that UFO's area real and present a threat to humanity's future. He actually said on my show that he felt "a possible alien invasion may pose a greater threat to humanity than global warming"!

Lionel and his wife Patricia have published a number of very well written and presented books which I recommend you all read.

Philip Gardiner – is the man they call the "real life Indiana Jones" because of his world travels chasing things like the Ark of the Covenant. His books include Gnosis and The Serpent Grail – and are essential additions to your book collection.

Philip is not someone easily convinced by myth and legend and when he says he believes the Ark of the Covenant to exist and to be a real phenomena, I readily believe him.

Philip is also the organizer of The Forbidden Knowledge Conference, where he brings together some of the greatest strange phenomena, researchers in the world in a fantastic one day conference in Stoke on Trent. I for one will definitely be there – I wouldn't miss that for the world.

Dr. Karen Ralls – is a leading researcher in the Knights Templar and Rosslyn Chapel and whatever you may have heard before about the historic Knights and their connections with the Sinclair's and Scotland – you need to read some of her work before making any conclusions.

Karen is another author who came onto the show and immediately caused me to rethink some of the myths and legends I had heard about the Templars, and like me she has visited many of the historic sites associated with them.

Riley Martin – believes that at the age of 8 he was abducted by aliens and taken to "a mother ship near the planet Saturn". Now whilst I have difficulty in believing the story – the way he delivers it does make you pause for thought.

Riley was a farm-hand who admits to being fairly "uneducated" – yet after the alleged abduction now has a very scientific mind and an understanding of matters that would baffle most of us. Could there be any truth in his story?

He has now gone on to get his own radio show on Howard Stern's Sirius Radio Network, and whether you believe his story or not – he is one of the most entertaining and listened to guests I have had on my show.

Ronnie Millione – is the "gadgets guy" for TAPS (The Atlantic Paranormal Society) the team featured in Sky's hit TV series Ghost Hunters. He has a very technical and design background and came onto the show to tell me about how he is working on recreating The Philadelphia Experiment.

For those of you who do not know about this experiment – it is said that the US Government tried to make a warship disappear, thus making it invisible to the enemy. The result however, includes claims that they traveled in time, personnel were driven to madness, and some were even fused into the very metal of the ship when it reappeared. It is without a doubt, one of the most fascinating experiments of our time.

Ronnie is also working on a time-travel experiment, and I found him to be knowledgeable, entertaining and someone who may just be at the very forefront of the next stage of paranormal research.

Beth Vegh – is not a name many of you may know, but she came to my attention through the Above Top Secret Forums (www.abovetopsecret.com) where she claimed STARGATES ARE REAL! Well as someone who believes stargates could answer a lot of unsolved historical questions, I got her on the show.

Her research was very strong, and she quoted many things within her findings that link to biblical quotes. Whilst she did not deliver any firm proof of the existence of these gateways, she certainly put forward a lot of strong evidence and I advise you all to seek her out on the Internet and watch for further developments.

Ralph Harvey – is the leader of the Order of Artemis and a self-confessed witch. He is a very intelligent and articulate man, who speaks very positively about magic and the good work that witches do around the world.

I have had the pleasure of meeting Ralph on a number of occasions and have found him to be very open about his work, and very respected in the community.

Ralph has been a guest of the programme several times now, and is always very popular with listeners. He talks about his own coven in Sussex and how they include everything from solicitors and policeman to office workers and shop-keepers

Elizabet – joined my show as our regular psychic as part of the sponsorship deal with Haunting Breaks, but she has developed into one of my most listened to and loved guests.

Each week she conducts an ESP and Telepathy test with the audience, often with great success, and her subjects for discussion always get a great response from the audience. She probably gets more e-mails than any other guest on the show.

Her psychic skills are without question – having constantly worked on investigations with Haunting Breaks and giving correct information that she could not have known about beforehand.

She also claims to be able to travel astrally and visit places she has never been to before, yet tell you all about them in great detail.

Ellie Crystal – is another regular guest on my show – and has probably the most visited pro-paranormal web site in the world with over a million hits a day! (www.crystalinks.com)

Ellie took part in a mass healing project with me and the listeners to see if we could speed up the recovery of Wayne Rooney's broken foot in time for the 2006 world cup.

She has a great knowledge of many things paranormal including spirituality, healing and of course crystals. Check out her web site when you get the opportunity.

Bart Sibrel – another of my favorite guests on the show. He claims he has PROOF that man never went to the moon in 1969, and sent me a DVD with the evidence he had collated. Penny and I sat and watched the documentary and it honestly made us believe he was correct in his claims. (See www.moonmovie.com)

Bart has spent many years collating his evidence and claims that he received the wrong clips from NASA when asking for some film footage – what they allegedly sent him was not meant to be seen by anyone and was marked top secret. It shows what Bart claims to be absolute proof of the faking of several very well known photographs.

I ask you all to buy the DVD and make up your own mind.

Belzebuub – yes, a very unusual name but a very entertaining and educational guest. He showed me that astral travel is something we can all do and he runs courses on-line at NO COST where you can train the art of movement out of body.

I am always intrigued when things like this are offered FREE as if they are not making money from it – they must really be doing it for the love and belief.

I am actually taking the course as I write this book, and should I get the opportunity to write a follow-up, maybe I will be able to tell you all the results.

Michael Mott – was recommended to me by a friend and paranormal researcher Brian Allen and he really got me thinking.

Michael spoke about Sasquatch (Bigfoot) and other mythical creatures that he believes exist in underground caves and caverns.

He also spoke about aliens possibly already being here in bases under the sea and below ground, and said that maybe we look up to the stars when we should in fact be looking down below us.

Could for instance – the strange things that occur in the Bermuda Triangle be because of an under sea alien civilization?

Well it certainly makes you think.

Chris Robinson – is known to many as "the Dream Detective". He has precognitive dreams almost to order. Chris claims that he chooses what he wishes to dream of before he goes to sleep and can even solve crimes for the Police in this manner.

I have tested Chris on a couple of occasions, including a weekend at the Theatre Royal in Margate, and he sealed the results of his dream the night before we went in an envelope which was opened on completion of the investigation. The results were 100% correct and he had not been told where he was going or even to which part of the country from his home in Bedfordshire.

He says that he informed the authorities days before the July 7th London bombings of what was going to happen yet nobody took him seriously. Think how many lives would have been saved if they had?

Maurice Gross – was the lead investigator into the Enfield Poltergeist case, one of the most incredible documented paranormal cases in history.

Maurice personally witnessed beds rising into the air, furniture moving across a room and a child talking in an old man's voice, which when checked, appeared to be coming from the back of the child's throat rather than from the mouth.

Maurice also witnessed poltergeist activity at Charlton House in London, where he says he heard an "explosion" as a cup fell to the floor. He tried everything to recreate that sound, breaking much crockery along the way – but never got a sound anything like what he witnessed that night. It later turned out that the cup was NOT from the building and appeared to "aport" from nowhere.

Nita Grant – is a team leader for the Phantom or Fraud Project, but we often refer to her as "the Oracle" as she is so knowledgeable in all things paranormal.

In one of two interviews she has done for the show, she spoke about alien abductions and the cases of sexual encounters between humans and aliens. It was a very frank and forthright interview, she certainly didn't hold back when discussing sexual content and orgasms.

She also pointed out that in cases where there appeared to be evidence of actual alien abduction, there was an actual change in the alleged abductee's alpha-wave patterns in the brain.

Nita is convinced that alien abductions really HAVE taken place and whilst a good percentage of claims are unsubstantiated, there are many cases that seem to provide solid evidence of this phenomena.

Gina Allan – nearly got me banned form the US radio syndication circuit. She is a world renowned psychic and sex counselor whom I met at the Spiritual Tides Festival in Kent in 2006. On the show, she claimed she could tell the size of a man's penis purely by talking to him and studying facial features. She also spoke openly about sex and orgasm's – something that provided great ratings for the show but included some words apparently still banned from broadcast in the USA.

I was so impressed with Gina's open style and ability to put across her case, that I gave her a sex and relationships show on Net Talk Radio. Do tune in when you get the chance.

Jean Kelford – is another spiritual medium and author, yet for some reason she stood out from many of the others I have had on the show. A lot of what she said seemed to make so much sense to me, and she put it across in a manner that was easy to understand and I believe she opened the minds of many listeners that night.

Strangely, I channeled some information for her live on the show and she was quite surprised when I described someone she knew very well, now in spirit.

Mark Macy – is an ITC and EVP investigator from the USA. ITC is the study if ghostly images seen under controlled conditions on a TV screen showing just "white noise" and EVP is the recording of what is claimed to be the voices of the dead.

Mark played some incredibly clear EVP recordings live on the show, including what he claims to be the voice of famous EVP researcher Konstantin Raudive who wrote the ground-breaking book Breakthrough all about EVP research.

Mark has also been working on "spirit photography" using a device which seems to show a different face super-imposed on the subject being photographed. Could this really be faces of the dead?

Patrick McNamara – is a physical medium, someone who claims to be able to manifest ectoplasm, photoplasm and full body spiritual entities. I was so intrigued at the work he was doing I set up a series of experiments to put physical mediumship to the test.

At the time of writing this book we have only just completed the first of these experiments, but I am convinced that he has some amazing gifts and am looking forward to further experiments with him and my team.

Marion Dampiere Jeans – is a Danish medium and clairvoyant, who my listeners voted as their favorite guest of 2005.

Marion was keen to promote the folklore, myths and legends of the Nordic countries, and told us some fascinating stories about things she has witnessed as far afield as Iceland, Greenland and in Scandinavia.

She is a gifted medium and is also now part of our physical mediumship experiment.

Brian Allen – is a paranormal and UFO researcher, and came onto my show to talk about his research at Rosslyn Chapel in Scotland. He has been working with sound experiments there using what he calls "the Devils Chord" - a musical note that he believes may open a dimensional doorway.

Brian has just published his first book, and also told us about some of the UFO encounters that he has researched.

One guy who I am not going to name – came onto my show talking about the "second coming of Christ" and for the first forty minutes sounded very rational before then announcing that the messiah was in fact the drug LSD! Needless to say he was invited back for a second airing.

I regularly get e-mails about "prophets" and other people claiming the second coming, but very few make it onto the programme after research. Who knows – one day I may even get to interview the real guy on his return "laughing out loud".

Stanton Friedman – is a world recognized expert on the Roswell UFO incident and spoke openly about what he believed really happened on that day in New Mexico.

He provided what he called "new evidence" to back-up claims that a UFO crashed there, and he put forward some convincing arguments. Roswell to me is much like the Rendlesham Forest incident in that the explanations from government sources and skeptics seem very lightweight and seem to provide less actual evidence than those from the other side of the fence.

Nick Pope – is one of my favorite regular guests on the show. He is the former UK government UFO investigator – a real life X-Files Fox Mulder.

Nick admits to being very skeptical about the existence of UFO's at the start of his research but is now absolutely convinced of their existence.

He is always a very popular guest who states his case very eloquently and is extremely popular with the show's listeners.

These are just a small handful of the excellent guests I have had on my show – and I'm sure many will return alongside the many new guests yet to come. Tune in every Friday 9:00 p.m. – midnight UK time online at www.nettalkradio.co.uk. See also www.nowthatsweird.co.uk

Thirty One
Conclusions

I am going to start this chapter with the obvious statement – that evidence does not define proof of the existence of the paranormal – but the more evidence we gain between us – the nearer we come to proving our case.

Let's remind ourselves of the evidence to date:-

Experiments seem to indicate that dowsing does work. I have tested many dowsers under controlled conditions, and the success rate has been over 80%.

Our research seems to indicate that some "orbs" show intelligence, thus ruling out dust, moisture or other air-born particles as a skeptical argument.

Constant monitored and reported cases of clairvoyants and mediums correctly giving information that they could not have known beforehand, rules out coincidence as an explanation of the "gifts".

Near-Death experiences show a constant likeness to other reported out-of-body phenomena, and on far too many occasions the reports from people reported to be physically dead at the time, show that they had an awareness and/or consciousness of events after the body was in that death state.

Far too many cases of paranormal investigations have noted a number of different instruments confirming the activity at the time, such as an EMF meter going off, a sever temperature change, an orb caught on camera or video, and a clairvoyant or medium describing a presence.

Sightings of ghosts in particular premises are too alike to be an "illusion". People who have no knowledge of a particular haunting often report seeing a particular figure in great detail, also witnessed by many other visitors.

Cases are now becoming more common of people materializing their own dreams by planning and seeing their future clearly enough. It is said that numerous celebrities have used this technique commonly known as "cosmic ordering" to achieve their dreams. Do we then create our own reality around us daily?

Crisis apparitions – another area of reports that bear incredible likenesses from all over the world usually at the time of an accident or death of a close friend or relative.

These are just a few examples of the evidence we hear about almost every day of the week.

It is my opinion that we all posses the gift of ESP or Telepathy, although the greatest percentage of us have no idea how to tap into it. Have you ever gone to pick the phone up just before it rings, or thought the doorbell was going to ring just before it did? Have you ever thought "oh I must ring my Mum" and then she rings you before you pick the phone up? Or have you ever had that chilling feeling that something was wrong and then the phone rings with some bad news? All of these things could be described as episodes of telepathy or ESP.

What about telekinesis? Have you ever sat down and tried to make something move purely with the power of your mind? I actually DID IT once whilst sitting in the bath and concentrating on a hairbrush on top of the toilet cistern. It had been on there all day without moving, yet as I channeled energy to it and imagined what it would feel like to be that hairbrush and imaging it moving –it suddenly moved and fell to the floor! Coincidence or telekinesis? To date I have not been able to repeat that success – but I remain convinced that there was no other way that brush could have moved the way it did.

So what about these parallel dimensions? Are we crossing over to their dimensions without knowing and appearing as a ghost? Are they appearing here in ethereal form? If these dimensions do indeed exist, then how can we live so very close without full proof of their existence?

It is always difficult when coming to conclusion based purely on small amounts of evidence, but no proof, but then the paranormal is not an exact science.

I believe that to take the research further forward, we need more new instruments of measurement to confirm things such as "Earth energies" actually exist. We also need different frequency infrared cameras to try to define the exact frequency that these entities can be seen in.

Furthermore, to test out of body experiences and near-death experiences, we need photographic equipment capturing the energy leaving the body and returning to it in confirmation of the times stated by the volunteer.

We should also now be working with hospitals and nursing homes, with discreet cameras to see if we can capture "orbs" leaving the body at the point of death of a patient. Yes, it's a controversial thing to suggest, but only with enough evidence, can we state our case as proven.

What about "haunted houses" – is there such a thing or is everywhere haunted? How do we test this theory? Well we could start by asking all of you to regularly photograph your home, especially if you feel anything may be present, also to try EVP experiments on a regular basis, and check any CCTV footage of your house each morning, you never know what you may find.

UFO's – are they coming from within our planet from under the sea in places like the Bermuda Triangle, or from a parallel universe, or are they from "outer-space"? Do they exist – is there enough evidence to "prove" their existence as yet?

What about extra-terrestrials? Many believe they are already here amongst us – perhaps its THEM that create the crop circles delivering messages into space?

Inter-dimensional beings – how would you identify one? They may look just like us – so how would we know?

David Icke says that he believes there are "reptilians" here on Earth living as humans – but he believes that on numerous occasions he has seen one changing. He also says he has been "scanned" from head to foot – could there be some truth in this? Should we be so quick to dismiss his theories? He has been on my radio show a couple of times now, and a lot of what he says makes an awful lot of sense.

What about the alleged "Illuminati"? Does a "super-race" exist here on Earth that controls the world, our leading politicians and every move we make? Is there a higher eschelon way beyond the highest Masons etc.? Is it just a conspiracy theory or are we really governed by 6 or 7 very powerful bloodlines?

What about the idea that the Holy Grail is in fact a direct blood-line of Jesus Christ? Did he marry Mary Magdalene or is this yet more fiction put forward by clever authors?

One question I would ask you all to consider, is why are so many sci-fi movies providing us with information that seems so close to a possible truth? Is it just creative minds at work, or are they tapping into a universal consciousness that is giving them information of something that actually already exists, or WILL exist in the future? One thing is for certain, for every new answer we gain, this answer itself produces another ten questions.

I am not here to change your mind or convince you that my research PROVES anything, I am here to open your mind to at least THINK and maybe accept that all is not quite as you had previously thought – and that some things currently DEFY rational or logical explanation. Just maybe the Dead ARE talking to us!

Reality is what you make it

LIFE CHANGING BOOKS AND DVDS BY REALITY PRESS

Tranceformers, Shamans of the 21st century
by Dr. John. J. Harper
foreward by Dr. Bruce Lipton
362 pages, $19.95 USD
isbn 0-9777904-0-1

The true story of this author's contact with a deceased physicist colleague that forced him to confront spiritual dilemmas we all face: Who are we? Why are we here? Where are we going? After 10 years of extensive research, the author derived that Trance---the method employed by the shaman is the doorway to the fifth dimensional field of cosmic consciousness.

Montauk Babies
(the many lives of Al Leedskalnin)
(the many lives of Al Leedskalnin)
by O.H. Krill
edited and illustrated by John Malloy
111 pages, 17.95 USD
isbn 0-9777904-2-8

"The past, present and future will merge into a finite point and no-one, I mean NO-ONE knows what the outcome will be, we must prepare the people for the coming change". Al Leedskalnin tells it like it is just days prior to the year 2012. While scientist Peabody Freeman and Al are on 'accident duty', the world outside has no idea that the end is near.

STEIGERWERKS CLASSICS SERIES!

Revelation, The Divine Fire
by Brad Steiger
258 pages, 19.95 USD
isbn 09777904-7-9

A Biblical prediction says "In the latter days, your sons and daughters shall prophesy." Brad Steiger has communicated with literally hundreds of individuals who claim to have received messages directly from God, or from spacemen, angels, spirit guides, or other superhuman entities and has documented these experiences in this SteigerWerks Classic. Revelation, The Divine Fire rings more profound and true than when first published in 1973.

Gnosis, the Secret of Solomon's Temple Revealed
DVD
Find the true secret of the Knights Templar and the mysteries of the ancients. This is the story that has been kept from the ears of mankind for too long. You cannot truly live until you have Gnosis.

* The truth at the heart of ancient Freemasonry
* Who were Solomon and Sheba?
* The ancient and sacred nature of our quantum existence

57 minutes 24.95 USD

Secrets of the Serpent, In Search of the Sacred Past
by Philip Gardiner
156 pages, 17.95 USD
isbn 0-9777904-3-6

Philip Gardiner reveals the world's most mysterious places were once sacred to the Serpent Cult. The history and mythology of the so-called reptilian agenda and alien visitation in ancient times now has a solid opponent. In this book the author reveals the real "bloodline" spoken of by Dan Brown in the Da Vinci Code.

Your Immortal Body of Light
by Mitchell Earl Gibson, M.D.
126 pages, 17.95 USD
isbn 0-9777904-5-2

Dr. Gibson was Chief Resident in Psychiatry at a large inner city medical center when he began his journey, expanding his consciousness using meditation. On his quest, he actually encounters an ancient 'god of healing' known as Djehuti (pronounced Dee-jan-tee), or Thoth. Both fascinating and chilling this is not your everyday spiritual awakening story.

All Online Orders receive a
FREE Reality Entertainment CD sampler
to order go to
www.reality-entertainment.com/books.htm

toll free order desk 1-866-585-1355

for wholesale inquries contact info@reality-entertainment.com
coming soon Reality Audio Books
featuring the Voice of **Brad Steiger**,
world renowned author

Secrets of the Serpent: In Search of the Sacred Past
DVD
Eons ago, an ancient serpent cult dominated mankind. Then, a great battle ensued and Christianity stamped it's authority on the face of the planet. Now, the real religious history of the world can be told. Philip Gardiner for the first time reveals:

* The world's most mysterious places were once sacred to the serpent cult.
* The secret of the Holy Grail and Elixir of Life
* The history and mythology of the so-called reptilian agenda

54 minutes 24.95 USD

Reality Press is a
division of
Reality Entertainment

www.reality-entertainment.com/books.htm

Printed in the United States
79742LV00003B/22-42